D&T ROUTES

TEXTILES

DESIGN & TECHNOLOGY 14-16

A TC Trust programme sponsored and
supported by the Royal College of Art,
the Esmée Fairbairn Trust,
the Garfield Western Foundation and the
Department for Education and Employment

Hodder & Stoughton

A MEMBER OF THE HODDER HEADLINE GROUP

The writing team

David Perry (Project Director), Louise T Davies (Deputy Project Director), Anthony R Booth (Assistant Project Director), Jim Sage (Assistant Project Director), Doris Massiah (Project Assistant), Alan Booth, Claire Buxton, Anne Constable, Corrine Harper, Mark Hudson, Dai James, Robin Pellatt, Rob Petrie, Brian Russell, Kalvin Turner (Teacher Fellows), Lesley Cresswell, Ali Farrell, Denise Fearon, Terry Fiehn, Dawn Foxall, Frances Geesin, Gill Greany, Clara Gregson, Maggie Grey, Jayn E Sterland, Wendy Thomas, Kathleen Twist and Sarah White.

Acknowledgements

Our special thanks to Lesley Cresswell (co-editor) for all the hard work on the designing section and glossary as well as helping the Project Team throughout the authoring of this book; and to all the Teacher fellows and their schools, particularly their colleagues, partners, friends and children who have supported them whilst they were writing to meet deadlines.

The Royal College of Art Schools Technology Project wishes to extend its thanks to the following for their help and support in the writing of this book: Kathleen Lund (Chief Executive) and her colleagues at the T.C. Trust, the Department for Education and Employment, Office for Standard in Education (OFSTED), The Royal College of Art and their representatives on the Project Management Group.

Many thanks to the following people and companies who helped with technical information and photographic material: Jane Bretherton, Michael Dicks and Irene Lynch (Shima Seiki); Michael Diesendorf (Husqvarna); Denise Fearon, Angela Gaskell, Frances Geesin, Ron Geesin, Tony Lay (Teknit), Chris Wilkinson, Michelle Wild, Nikki Young, Monica Zipper, Brentford School for Girls, Leeds University, NADCAT, Thomas Telford School, TIPs Schools, West Nottinghamshire College, Cheryl Playclothes, Coats Viyella, Courtaulds, D&E Textiles, DuPont, Emprex International, Douglas Gill, The Logo Carpet Company, Monarch Textiles, Northern Diver, Pilgrim Textiles, Samsonite, Scope, Speedo, The Sweater Shop, Welbeck UK.

The illustrations were drawn by: Tony Wilkins, Tom Cross, Joseph McEwan, Richard Duszczak.

The publishers would like to thank the individuals, institutions and companies listed right for permission to reproduce copyright photographs in this book. Every effort has been made to trace ownership of copyright. The publishers would be happy to make arrangements with copyright holders whom it has not been possible to contact.

Allan Cash, J. (22 top left, 68 bottom); Albany International Research Co. (90 top 2); Allsport/Al Bello (45); Allsport/Simon Bruty (37 left); Allsport/Mike Hewitt (34 bottom); Arcaid/Richard Bryant (35 middle right, 71 top right); Ashfield School (65 left); Batten, Bill (4 lower); Berlei (62 left); Birdair (58 top 3); Birdsall, John (10 both, 12 top left, 60 left, 62 top right, 86 top 4, middle right); Bleep 2000/The Sweater Shop (70); Boden, Gareth (3 both, 6, 8 middle left, lower left, 9 upper 3, 13 middle, 30 all, 31 all, 38, 39, 41); Bodo Rasch Architects (44); Brennand-Wood, Michael (27 top); Brookes and Vernon Design/Northern Diver (72); Brother UK (60 middle right, 78 left); Brown, Gerard (23 top); BTTG (66 top right); Burgess, Chris (7 middle, 8 top left, 20 top left, right, lower right, 21 lower right, 32 lower 3, 43 right, 61 top left, 63, 69, 71 left, 73 lower right, 76 right 2, 78 middle right, lower right, 79 left, 83 middle right); Capitol Public Relations/DuPont (28 top right, 28/29 lower, 42 right); Cheryl Playclothes (57 right); CND (24 left); Courtaulds Textiles (9 bottom); Dalf (80 left); Dennis Publishing (13 bottom); DuPont (36 top, 37 top right, 47 left, 53 left, 82, 92 left); Eco-labelling Board (46 right); Ellis, Martin I. (77 all); Emmerich/Berlon (8 middle right, lower right); Eurotech (79 lower right); Eye Ubiquitous (23 background); Ford UK (36 bottom); Gaskell, Angela (57 middle left, lower left); Geesin, Frances (29 top, 35 bottom left, 51 left, 54 top); Geesin, Ron (52 lower 2); Gerber Garment Technology (58 lower 3, 73 upper right); Gill, Douglas/Peter Bentley (21 middle); Greaney, Gill/Beauchamp College (26 all, 35 lower right, 40 lower right, 54 lower, 55 both, 56 all); Gregson, Clara/Thomas Telford School (2, 53 right, 61 lower 2); Grey, Maggie (25 top); Guzelian Photography (68 top); Heald & Co., James H. (66 left, middle right); HLCC (47 right); Hoechst (28 left); Hounsell, Pete (16 left); Imagination (43 left); JSA/Electrolux (79 top right); Koronka, Peter (16 top, bottom, 17 background); Lancashire, Neil (83 bottom 2); Lectra Systems (65 right, 76 left 2); Life File/David Kampfer (90 bottom left); Life File/Emma Lee (12 top right); Life File/Louise Oldroyd (17 middle); Linear Composites (89 upper right); Logo Carpet Co. (71 bottom right); MacWilliams, Irene (24 right 3, 25 background); Mainstream/Ray Main (5 background); Marie Claire/Mitchell Sams (40 middle right); McQueen, Alexander (34 top); Monarch Textiles (19); News International (51 top); Nottingham Trent University, Dept. of Fashion and Textiles (89 bottom right); PPL (22 lower left); Rex Features (22 lower left, lower right); Royal Armouries © The Board of Trustees of the Armouries (42 left); Safeline (80 middle right); Samsonite (67 lower right); SealSkinz (52 top); Shima Seiki (85 right all, 87); The Sweater Shop (33 background); Teknit (86 bottom right both); Thomas, Wendy/Simon Doughty (46); Thompson, Mrs C. (89 left); Trip/V. Kolpakov (85 left); Trip/H. Rogers (33 top, 60 top right, 80 bottom right); Twist, Kath/Shevington High School (59); U4ai (73 lower left); Welbeck UK (91, 92 right, 93 both); Whiting Associates, Elizabeth (35 top right); Zweigle, Prof. Herbert Henne (67 left).

British Library Cataloguing in Publication Data
A catalogue record for this title is available from The British Library

Student Book
ISBN 0 340 67391 5

First published 1998
Impression number   10 9 8 7 6 5 4 3 2 1
Year   2002 2001 2000 1999 1998

Teacher's Notes
ISBN 0 340 69734 2

First published 1998
Impression number   10 9 8 7 6 5 4 3 2 1
Year   2002 2001 2000 1999 1998

Typeset by Wearset, Boldon, Tyne and Wear
Printed in Hong Kong for Hodder & Stoughton Educational, a division of Hodder Headline Plc, 338 Euston Road, London NW1 3BH by Colorcraft, Hong Kong

Contents

Acknowledgements ii
Introduction 2

Designing and Making Assignments 4

In the mood 4
Pack-up and go 10
Fit and fun 16
Survival 22
Textiles talk 24
On the surface 26
Technical textiles 28
Crossing cultures 30
Made to order 32

Designing 34

What are textiles products? 34
Where do new ideas come from? 36
Market place demand 36
New situations 37
Redesigning to add value 37
Social and cultural influence 37
Generating ideas 38
How do textiles product designers work? 38
Starting points for your designing 38
Looking at existing products 39
In the style of . . . 40
Inspired by . . . other cultures 40
Experimenting with ideas 41
Thinking about . . .
Function 42
Style and colour 43
Cost and prices 44

Health and safety 45
The environment 46
Product life 47
Materials 48
Exploring textile techniques 53
Distressing techniques 54
Dyed and sculpted textiles 55
Machine embroidery 55
Appliqué and mola 56
Hand-made felt 56
Design research 57
Modelling and prototyping 58
Designing for manufacture 60
Communicating designs 61

Manufacturing 62

Taking ideas into production 62
Developing a manufacturing specification 64
Testing before production 66
Production planning 69
Different methods of production 71
Quality assurance and quality control 81
Team working in industry 83
Systems and control 85
The use of new technologies 89

The business of manufacturing 91

Who are the manufacturers? 91
Case study: Welbeck UK (technical textiles) 91

Index 94

Introduction

This book should be used with the *D&T Routes Core Book* which provides you with advice on how to organise and manage your work in design and technology. It will help you to analyse and evaluate products, and with your designing and manufacturing. It also will build the understanding of industrial approaches to manufacturing in a variety of materials which both GCSE D&T and GNVQ Manufacturing courses expect.

This book contains:

◆ three **Full Designing and Making Assignments** (**DMAs**) comprising a design and make challenge together with supporting focused tasks and case studies

◆ six **Outline DMAs** which present you with a design and make challenge and some starting points to help you get going

◆ **Designing and Manufacturing** sections with focused tasks, information and case studies to support your designing and making, and knowledge about industrial approaches

◆ a section on the **the business of manufacturing** which will help further develop your understanding of manufacturing. This is essential if you are following a GNVQ Manufacturing course but will also enhance your designing and making if you are on a GCSE D&T course.

Paul used binding wire for his textile structure. The decoration was made from fingerprints on sticky-backed plastic.

You can use the DMAs as they stand or to help you to develop your own projects.

There are five focus area books in the *D&T Routes* series: *Resistant Materials*; *Food Technology*; **Textiles**; *Control Products* and *Graphic Products*. You will find it useful to refer to the others in the series.

Design and Technology produces products in various materials but there are common features to the designing processes and manufacturing processes used. If you are following a GCSE course with a narrower focus you should firstly think about what is special to your focus area.

What is textiles technology?

Textiles technology provides you with exciting opportunities for creative design and manufacturing using flexible materials. You can try making and decorating materials to create 'fabulous fabrics'. You can use your experimental fabric work to make quirky new products. Textiles technology is demanding, exciting and fun!

This student used a design of coloured fleece and yarn in her felted fabric.

This student worked with a manufacturer of leisurewear to design and manufacture children's clothing for his company, Pins & Needles. This is his final working drawing.

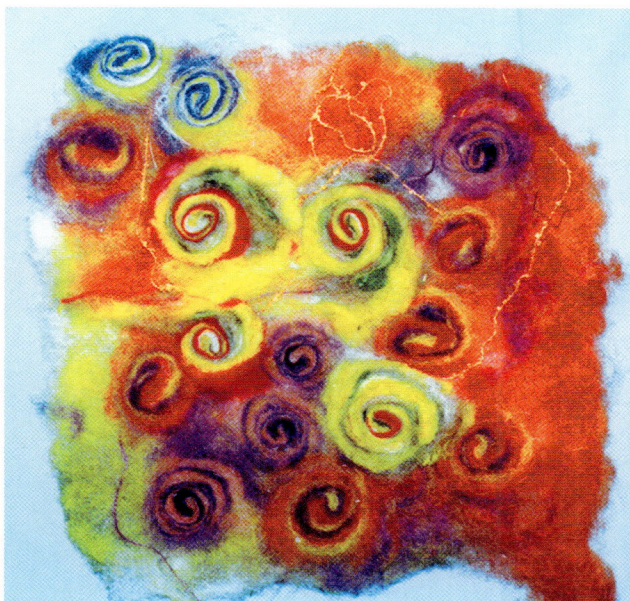

In the mood

Your challenge

Brightly coloured, textured or patterned fabrics can change the style or 'look' of a room. Fabric designers have to produce design ideas that are suitable for a wide range of interiors, such as a theatre entrance, a motel bedroom or a sports club restaurant. Choose a room in a location that is used by a specific client group and investigate the types of textile products used there. Look at the colours, styles and patterns of the fabrics.

Your challenge is to develop and make a **prototype fabric sample**, suitable for a co-ordinated range of textile products, designed for your chosen interior and client group. You will need to consider the scale of your design and how CAD could be used in its development.

Textile artist Lauren Shanley uses recycled materials in her colourful interiors.

Why this activity is useful

This project helps you understand how designers use colour, pattern and texture in fabrics to promote and sell style and comfort to a variety of clients.

It will help you find out how designs can be used in different sizes or scales to develop co-ordinated fabrics for a range of textile products. You will learn how **design influences** help the designer.

You will have the opportunity to learn about different processes needed to develop woven, knitted or printed fabrics.

You can learn how CAD is used by designers to develop sample fabrics for trialling a client's textile product.

Values issues

◆ Many designers use **image** and **lifestyle** to promote and sell their products. Discuss how consumers are encouraged to buy products because of their image. Identify a particular product and evaluate its relationship with a way of life or lifestyle.

◆ Designers use the influence of other cultures to develop their ideas. Do we exploit or promote these cultures by making use of their traditional design styles? Collect ideas and explain how they have been influenced by other cultures.

◆ The manufacture of fabrics can cause pollution when waste water is released into rivers. What can be done to minimise the disposal of waste products?

To be successful

You will need to:
★ research one type of room interior that is used by a specific group of clients. Look at the range of textiles to help you formulate a precise fabric specification.
★ use your knowledge of the way that fabrics are designed in terms of colour, pattern and texture and make use of an art or design 'style' to influence your fabric development
★ use CAD to help you develop your ideas
★ produce a fabric sample that could be used to make a range of different textile products
★ evaluate your prototype fabric and assess its appeal in your chosen interior.

How to get going

▸ Identify an interior of a public building that you will be able to research. Make a detailed survey of the way fabrics, the colour scheme, textures and patterns are used. Collect information about styles of fabric decoration and put together a storyboard of design influences for your client. Write a fabric specification, explaining how your fabric will suit a range of products in your interior.

▸ Generate a number of pattern ideas using computer software. Put pattern designs into repeats and try out colourways. Use trial print-outs to evaluate the size of the design. Use the final computer print-out as a guide for stencils.

▸ Produce a prototype fabric and evaluate its suitability for a co-ordinated range of products for the people using your chosen interior.

In the mood

Looking at existing products

Visit your chosen interior and survey the textiles products there. You could make a chart with headings like the one shown to record information about each product. Include a sketch of the fabric pattern with colour combinations.

- Note the overall style or mood of the room and the kind of person who would use it.
- Explain how this information will help you to make decisions about the kind of fabric that you would like to use in the room.

This student drew up a chart to record information about textile products.

SURVEY OF TEXTILE PRODUCTS – Hotel bedroom

	curtains	chair cover	duvet cover
What is fabric used for?	curtains	chair cover	duvet cover
What is fabric construction?	woven with print design	satin weave	
Fibre content?	100% cotton		poly-cotton
Fabric properties needed?		hard-wearing	
Fabric aftercare?	dry-clean		easy-care
Style or mood of room?	cosy with 'country' style		
Who uses the room?			
Colour scheme?	Blues and pinks		

Finding out about fabric design

Working with fabrics is exciting because the aesthetics or language of design, such as visual appearance and touch, can be used in a creative way. Fabric designers nearly always work with themes or 'stories' to influence their design and colour ideas.

Choose a theme such as 'Crazy Colour', 'Moody, Mysterious and Modern' or 'Planet Earth' and make a collection of colour and fabric swatches, yarn samples and magazine 'swipes' (pictures) showing styles of room interiors, images and textile products. Use these to create a moodboard to illustrate your ideas about your theme to suit the 'look' of your chosen interior and client type.

One student produced this moodboard to help develop ideas.

Looking at fabrics

The way a fabric is constructed or made affects its properties and how it is used. Look at some textile products. For each product state the fabric construction and properties.

I Find out how woven, non-woven, knitted and printed fabrics are manufactured.

- Disassemble a woven fabric to discover the weave construction and colour order of the warp and weft.
- Pull a non-woven fabric apart to see the entangled fibres.
- Examine a knitted fabric to see the construction and number of colours used.
- Check a printed fabric to find the pattern repeat and number of colours.

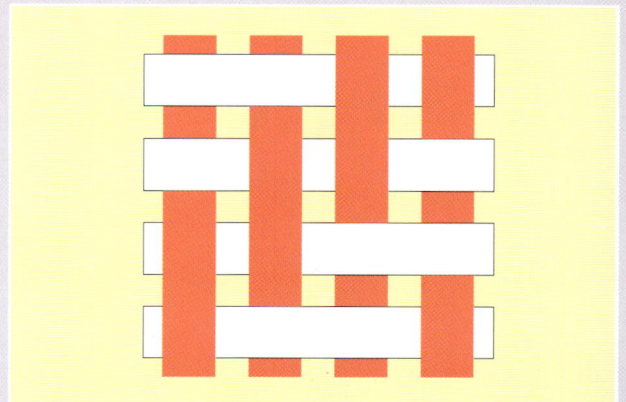

a) Woven fabrics can drape well, be hard-wearing and can be colour-woven or plain for printing on. They are suitable for seating, curtains, bedlinen and tableware.

Formulating a specification

Use your research work on interiors, your moodboard of design influences and your experimental work on fabric construction to help write your specification. You may like to produce a chart similar to the one on the right.

Specification for my prototype fabric

Type of interior	school reception area
Who uses it?	students, teachers, other adults
Textile product	curtains
Style or mood	modern
Design influence	the 1960s
Colour scheme	warm and colourful
Fabric type	
Production method	print
Fabric aftercare	

Looking at fabrics — continued

2 Produce experimental samples of woven, non-woven, knitted or printed fabrics. Have fun!

■ Use coloured paper to trial weave constructions and colour combinations.
■ Use a card, frame or shaft loom to experiment with yarns, texture and colour.
■ Try making felt with woollen yarns.
■ Experiment with hand or machine knitting.
■ Try printing fabrics with polystyrene/cork or potato blocks.
■ Use a small screen and paper stencils to trial fabric prints.

Pippa Purser from Tuxford School experimenting with screen prints.

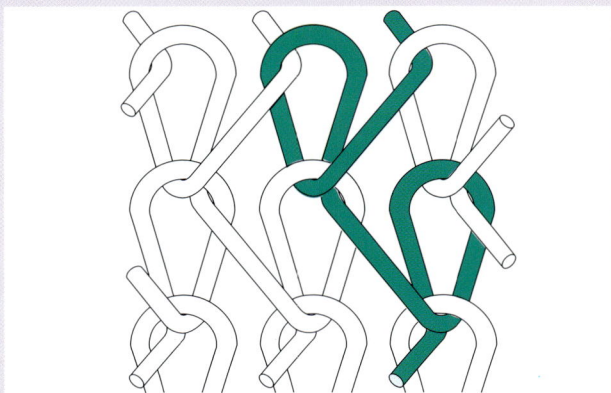

b) Warp-knitted fabrics are stretchy and can be used for fitted upholstery or curtains.

c) Non-woven fabrics are made from webs of tangled fibres, and can be used as carpet underlay or as interfacing in upholstery. This non-woven Lyocell is suitable for medical end uses.

In the mood

Generating ideas with CAD

Your experimental work on fabric construction, your specification and moodboard will help you develop your fabric ideas.

Ellana Brownhill from Tuxford School working on a CAD project.

Develop fabric ideas using computer software for print, knit or embroidery designs.

- Scan in drawings, sketches, ideas from your moodboard, photos, paper cut-outs, magazine/newspaper images, patterns and textures. Import images via a video camera or CD-ROM.
- Use CAD software to adapt and change images or colours, and to experiment with scale and proportion.
- Use CAD to rotate, mirror, resize or distort images to create a design motif.
- Use CAD to repeat your design motif as a border or all-over pattern.
- Try out your pattern in different colour combinations based on your moodboard colour palette.

Develop fabric ideas using computer software for weave designs.

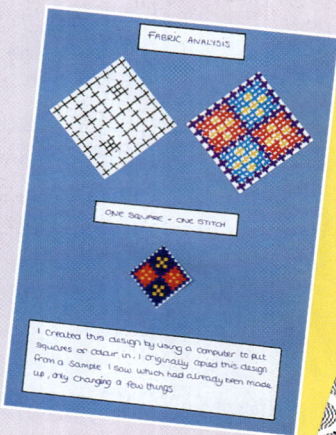

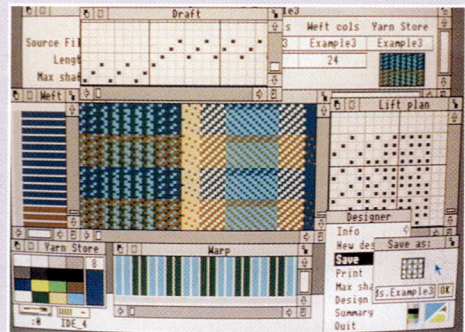

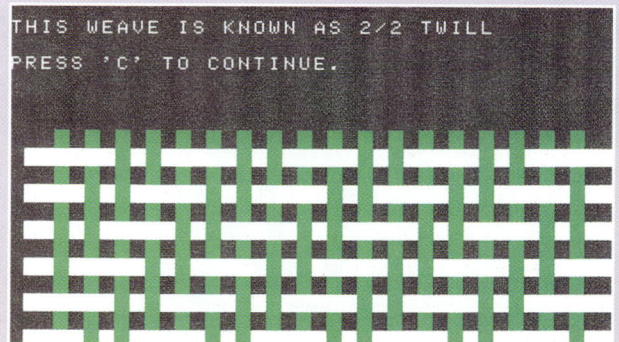

Weave designs can be tried out on screen, then exported to a loom for weaving.

- Use weave software to try out weave constructions like plain or twill.
- Try different colour combinations in the warp and weft.
- Experiment with your fabric design scale to simulate different yarn counts (thickness).

Outputting design ideas

Your CAD ideas can be output in a variety of ways.

- Print a linear design in small or large scale to evaluate its size on a product.
- Print a linear design to use as a stencil for appliqué, fabric painting, screen-printing or patchwork.
- Print your design in colour for use in presentation work
- Print on transfer paper, iron on to fabric, and use to make a sample product.
- Export to a cutter-plotter to cut separate colour stencils for screen-printing.
- Export to embroidery software, digitise the stitch information and output as embroidery.
- Export to knit software, convert into stitches and rows, simulate a knitted fabric, transfer to a knitting machine and knit.
- Export weave design information to a numerically-controlled loom and weave samples or larger fabric pieces.

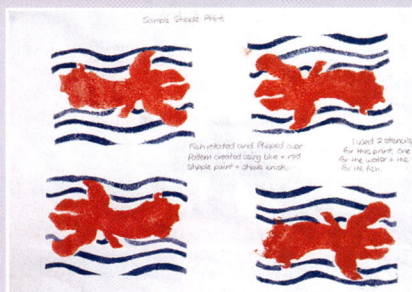

Prototyping and evaluating

1 Produce a fabric **prototype** to suit your intended textile product and interior. You could:

- mount your fabric as part of a presentation to show clients
- produce drawings of co-ordinating textile products using the fabric in differing scales or colours.

If there is time you could make a simple sample product using your fabric.

2 Use your fabric specification to make a list of things which are important for a successful textiles product in the interior of your choice. What would someone using the room want it to be like? A successful product and interior will meet the needs of the user. How are you going to **evaluate** the things on your list?

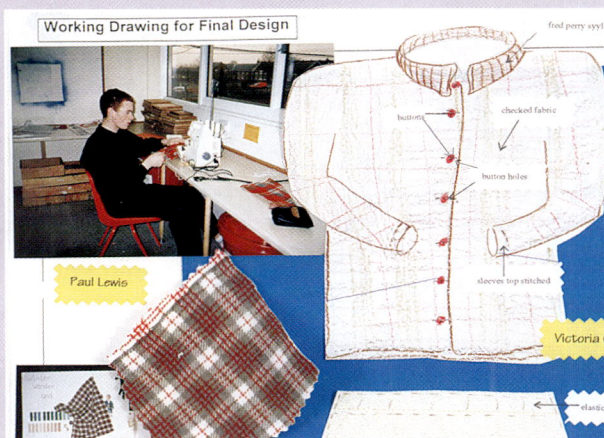

Case study: Courtaulds Textiles

Courtaulds Textiles design studio use CAD to develop printed fabric designs. These can be output directly to the printer for sampling fabric lengths. Then a sample garment can be made up and shown to the client for approval.

Using CAD software to model ideas means that a design can be changed at any stage of development. It is possible to work from the design concept to the sample garment in less than eight hours.

Pack-up and go

Many people are on the move as part of their work. They do not have a permanent desk that they use every day, but work in a number of places taking their equipment and papers with them. This is called **hot desking**. You do this too, at school – moving from classroom to classroom, to the library, to the computer room, and taking your work home. So you know what it is like to move from place to place!

Your challenge is to design and make a **prototype** of a useful storage item that a person who has to carry their equipment with them could use. Design it so that the item can be manufactured in high volume and the basic design could be personalised or decorated to appeal to a range of users.

Why this activity is useful

The item you are designing will be useful in the changing world of working from home and hot desking. This challenge gives you the opportunity to examine how people work, what their daily lives are like, and what they are required to carry with them to do their jobs.

It will extend your knowledge of choosing and testing appropriate materials for the function of the item, and reconciling difficult decisions about which material to choose (the need for durability or washability, protection of equipment, and so on) with considerations of cost, safety, ease of manufacture, aesthetics and appeal to the consumer.

Your making skills will be extended to produce a high-quality prototype, including pattern-cutting, joining and reinforcing fabrics, and decorating and personalising the product for different groups of people.

You will also learn about designing for manufacture in high volume.

Values issues

◆ Many people work from home or do not have permanent workplaces to go to. What are the social effects of this?

◆ What is meant by a nomadic lifestyle? Find out about other cultures and times where nomadic lifestyles were important. What is life like? Why is it necessary? What might we learn from their success to help us?

◆ Sometimes, when products are decorated for different groups of people, assumptions are made about the type of image different groups will like. When designing your product think carefully about the image you are portraying of the group you are designing for, and how accurately it reflects the group's make-up.

To be successful

★ Your item should be designed and made to a high standard. The prototype should be of good enough quality to present to a manufacturer as an example of a finished product.

★ You will have researched the situation and needs of the user and designed an item which is fit for its purpose. The fabrics and components used will have been chosen carefully, reconciling the demands of function, safety, aesthetics, costs and ease of manufacture.

★ You will have considered how the item will be manufactured, simplifying the number of parts to the design and process of making up.

★ The finished item should appeal to the user as being functional and attractive to use.

How to get going

▸ Research the situation carefully so that you are able to identify the needs of a particular group. Find out what items they carry with them and how flexible your design needs to be. Are there standard measurements for some items?

▸ Model your ideas in inexpensive materials. Gather the items that will be stored together (or use 'dummies' of similar dimensions) and try out your ideas with paper, card or scrap fabric.

▸ Decide what properties the fabrics will need to have (essential and useful). This will depend on the needs of the consumer and the situation in which the item is used. Find out about fabric properties and carry out fabric tests to help you choose the right materials.

▸ Using CAD/CAM could help you throughout the challenge.

Pack-up and go

Handyperson's work belt

This task is a quick activity for you to try before designing your own storage item. It is a mini-project which will help you understand some of the things you will have to think about later.

Design a belt for a person to carry his or her tools in from job to job.

- Firstly, find out as much as possible about the tools that the person will need in a usual day's work. Make a list of them and take some measurements.
- Collect images about the job they are doing and make visual studies as a starting point for your design ideas, such as colours, textures and shapes.
- What are the safety considerations – for the person wearing it and others around?
- How can you make it comfortable?
- What kind of fabric is needed and what fabric would be suitable? (Washable, waterproof, lightweight, durable?)
- Use your results and visual images to develop your design.

Researching situations and focusing

The handyperson's work belt is an example of just one of many situations for which you could design. The possibilities are endless! It will be helpful if you look at a number of different situations for which you may design a useful storage item. This will help you to decide which one to choose. You will then need to look at the particular requirements in more detail so that you can design something to meet them.

This student is starting to find out about a number of opportunities for design before researching a particular design need in more detail.

People	Situations in which they need storage items	Items to store	Features
Primary school children	at their desk		
computer operator	in office	disks	
business person	travelling from site to site	mobile phone, disks, stationery, photo portfolio	

Looking at existing products and adapting designs

This is another activity to give you some ideas before you start designing your storage item. Produce a basic design for a storage item where the function is determined by the type of fabric used.

For example, a pencil-case design could easily be altered into a jewellery roll through simply choosing a more decorative or luxurious fabric. The dimensions and design will remain unaltered, while the type of fabric is changed to suit the uses.

Making the product suitable for the user

Understanding the needs of the person you are designing for is very important. There is no point in designing a product that no one will buy. You will need to collect information about the users' needs, interests and preferences. Some designers present client profiles as moodboards.

- a list of the things they need to store, with technical information such as their size and nature. Are they fragile, will they bend? will one item affect other items?
- how the storage item will be used
- when it will be used
- how it will work
- what features are important (strength, durability, protection, colour, ease of use, appearance, price, flexibility of use?).

As well as finding out about people's likes and dislikes, you will need to develop a clear specification which includes the following:

Choosing the right materials

It is unlikely that your storage item will be made from just one material. You will probably need to choose a combination of carefully selected fabrics and components. You may find it helpful to look at the materials used in other storage items and analyse why they have been chosen.

continued page 14

Pack-up and go

Choosing the right materials — continued

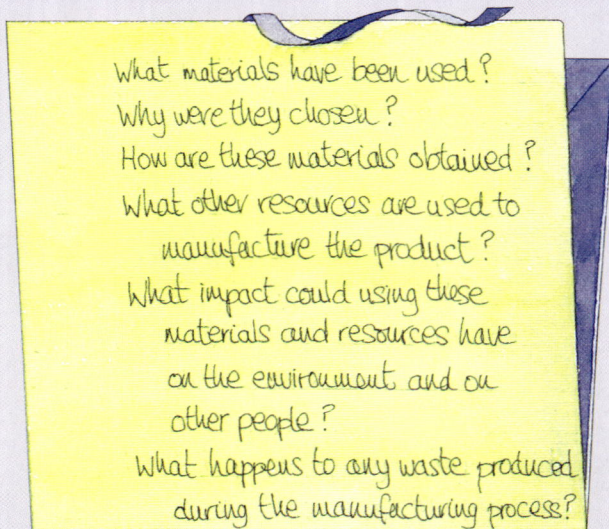

What materials have been used?

Why were they chosen?

How are these materials obtained?

What other resources are used to manufacture the product?

What impact could using these materials and resources have on the environment and on other people?

What happens to any waste produced during the manufacturing process?

When you consider what materials you will need for your design, think about these questions.

- What are the handling or working characteristics of the materials you need for your design to be successful?
- Which properties are essential and which are useful?
- What materials are suitable for this purpose?
- Will you need to use combinations of materials (such as layers) or use different materials for different parts of your design (for example, outside and inside)?
- How much material will you need?
- What quality of material should you use?
- How much will your materials cost?
- What will be the cost implications of quality (will people be willing to pay for the best quality materials in this product)?
- Are there are standard components or ready-made parts you could use?

Modelling

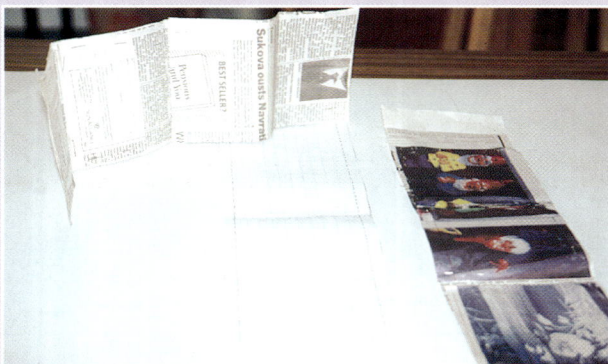

Modelling can help you in a number of ways. To stimulate ideas:

- gather the things to be stored by your customer, and use inexpensive fabrics or thin card to try out some different ways of organising them
- use the card or fabric pieces to make a pattern for your design
- use a computer to draw your initial ideas, or sketch them by hand.

To develop and refine your ideas:

- make a mock-up of your design in cheaper fabric and test it out against your specification to look for areas of improvement. Use your mock-up to present your ideas to others for their reactions
- use a computer to try different colourways and decorative features

- draw the pattern pieces for your storage item on the computer, look for ways to simplify the pattern so that it is easier to manufacture, and find the best pattern lay to minimise the amount of waste fabric.

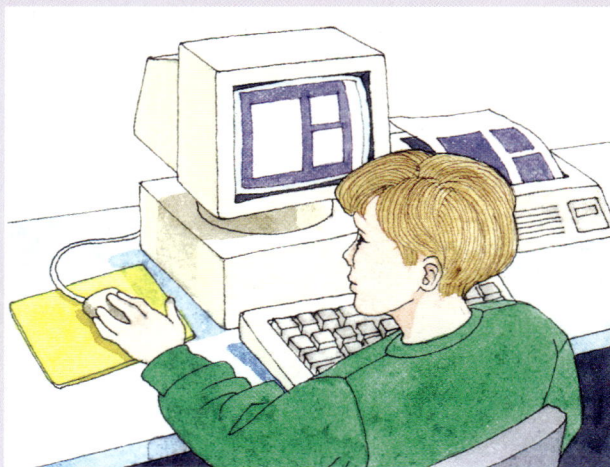

Use a computer spreadsheet to work out the cost of variations on your design. You might include materials and production time. Is this within the price range indicated in your specification? Will the consumer be willing to pay extra for highly-decorated articles which may be more costly to manufacture? Use the spreadsheet to model alternative ideas.

Personalising and variations on a theme

As you are designing for a particular target group, your design and decorative features should reflect them. How will you find out what people really like in your user group?

- Think carefully about the image of the group you are portraying in your design.
- How accurately does this reflect the make-up of the group you are designing for?
- Would it be possible to use your original idea and personalise it for different groups by using decorations and adding pieces to a basic design?

Batch production

You have been asked to design a storage item with a basic design that can easily be adapted for various types of customer. This adaptation should be through a simple change of colour and the addition of decoration. There are many decorative techniques that you can use, including embroidery, appliqué, dyeing and printing. You need to think carefully about the order of making the product.

- How far can the basic product be made up before variations need to start?
- When will be the best time to dye it?
- When will be the best time to embroider it?
- When will be the best time to print on it?

The diagram should help you to decide which design route to take. You can choose different techniques and select the order in which to complete each variation by using this chart.

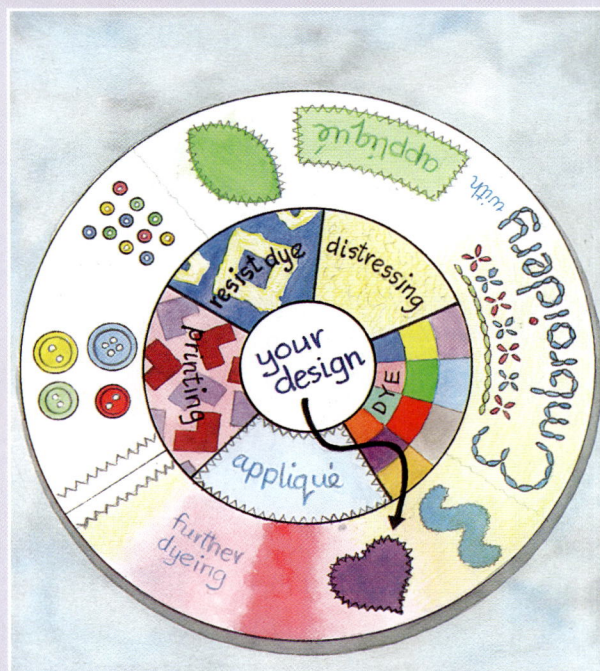

The arrow shows the route Tom has taken for his design. He has dyed his design to demand, and added an appliqué shape to personalise it.

Fit and fun

Your challenge

Whatever sport you like to do, it is important that you have the right kit to do it **safely**. Serious and fatal injuries to pedal cyclists, for example, account for almost ten per cent of road accidents. 'To be seen' is one of the recommendations of the Department of Transport. The right kit can help you to be seen – fluorescent by day, reflective by night.

Your challenge is to design a cycling safety garment or accessory suitable for people aged under 16 to wear when cycling on the road. **Safety** should be a priority, and you should incorporate the use of fluorescent and reflective materials . The garment you design should make cycling safer and young people must want to wear it.

Why this activity is useful

You will become more aware of new fabrics and their special characteristics.

You will need to consider the functional aspects of the garment as well as the fashion appeal.

This project will enable you to explore different ways of joining fabrics and ensuring that they remain waterproof.

It will help you to understand the difficulties encountered by industry when mass-producing garments with such restrictions.

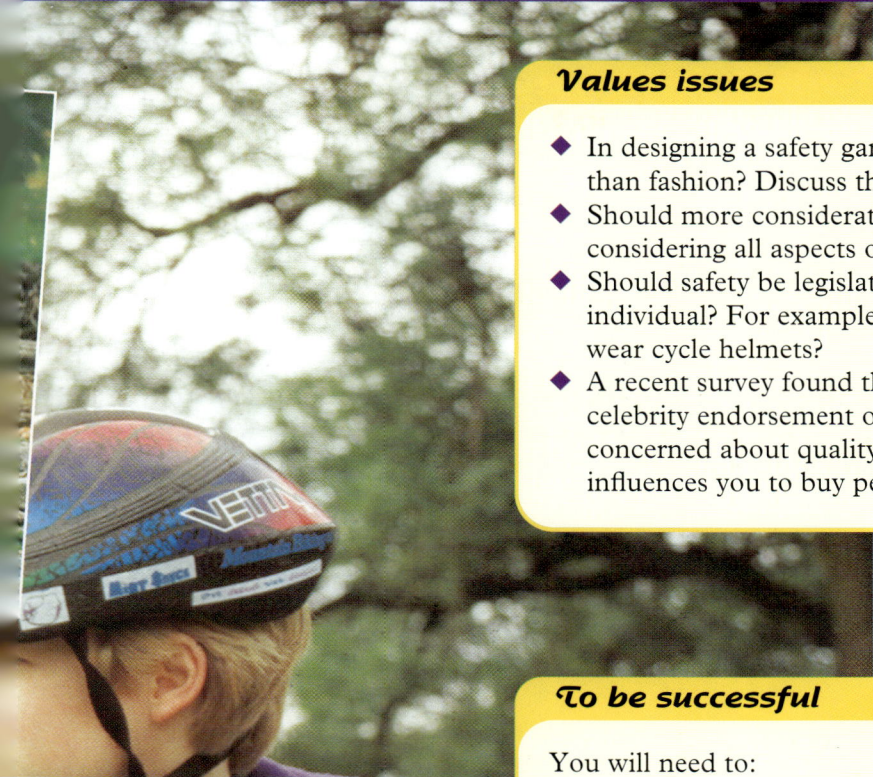

Values issues

- In designing a safety garment, is function more important than fashion? Discuss this in a group.
- Should more consideration be given to cyclists when considering all aspects of road safety?
- Should safety be legislated for or should it be left to the individual? For example, should it be made law for cyclists to wear cycle helmets?
- A recent survey found that most people are not influenced by celebrity endorsement of sports clothing. They are more concerned about quality, style, price and colour. What influences you to buy performance clothing?

To be successful

You will need to:

- ★ investigate British safety requirements for cycling safety garments
- ★ research the range of cycle-wear available in the shops
- ★ explore suitable fabrics and fastenings, and ways of joining and shaping
- ★ make sure that the design and shape of the garment or accessory takes into account safety, comfort and function
- ★ experiment with different joining techniques, thinking about strength, waterproofing and comfort
- ★ consider the market appeal – your item must make it safer for a cyclist because they can be seen, and they will want to wear it because it has been well designed and made.

How to get going

- You may need to contact specialist fabric suppliers. Make sure you allow plenty of time for this.
- Research the market.
- Produce a range of drawings incorporating the different criteria.
- Develop a moodboard and evaluate your designs.
- Make a prototype to test your design.
- Decide upon the materials and techniques, and produce samples prior to making.

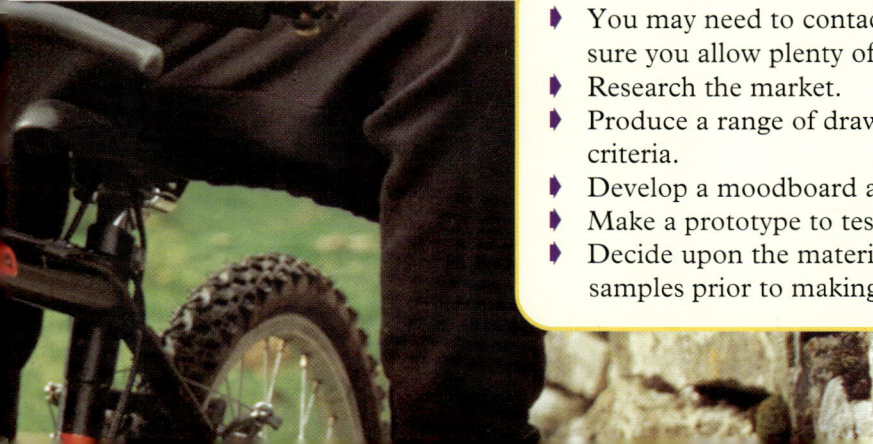

Fit and fun

Sportswear — sporting style

Sportswear is one of the fastest developing textile apparel areas. Traditional sports clothing from the 1950s and 1960s became known as **activewear** in the 1980s. Now the interest in fitness and activities like jogging or aerobics has led to the 1990s being called the 'decade of the body'. Leggings and body-hugging clothes have become possible through the use of new fibres and stretchy fabrics. Most recently, microfibres have enabled the development of performance fabrics for specialist sports. Technical innovation is predicted to expand the sportswear influence well into the next century.

What are the most popular sports activities?

Put the following list of sports or leisure activities (add any more of your choice) into what you consider is their order of popularity for a specific age group. Then ask at least 20 people in that group which is their favourite sporting activity. Compare the results. What have other students found out? Is there a difference between male and female preferences, or between different age groups? Collate your research into a database and print out results for age groups and gender preferences.

swimming	rambling	aerobics
jogging	racquet sport	snooker
golf	training	football
keep-fit	athletics	rugby
skiing	snowboarding	dancing
climbing	in-line skating	darts
cycling		

You can use the results of your research to identify your customer group more closely.

- Who takes part in cycling?
- What kind of people are they?
- What are their needs?
- What will they like?
- What is important to them?

What makes good cycle-wear?

Cycle-wear needs to provide a range of properties such as comfort, flexibility and protection against the heat, cold, wind, rain and perspiration. Look at items worn by cyclists. These will vary according to the season or time of year. You could collect this information as a group.

- What fabrics are used?
- Why have these particular fabrics, techniques and finishes been chosen?
- How is the item made?
- How many parts or components are there?

Draw up a table like this one to show your findings. You may also want to investigate how cycle-wear has changed over time and why this has happened.

What will be the important characteristics for your design? What features are essential, and what others might also be useful?

What makes good cycle-wear

Season used	Item	Performance requirement	Fabrics
Summer			
Autumn			
Winter			
Spring			

Looking at fabric properties

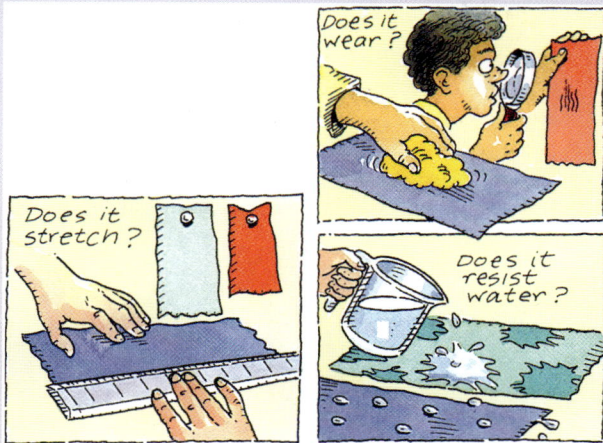

Does it wear?

Does it stretch?

Does it resist water?

Newark area				
Casualty type	day/ dark	1991	1992	1993
Child pedal cyclists	day	33	28	20
	dark	5	2	2
Adult pedal cyclists	day	31	37	29
	dark	7	8	11
Age unknown pedal cyclists	day	0	2	2
	dark	0	0	1
Total		76	77	65

What fabrics can you choose which are likely to fulfil your design criteria? Evaluate your selection of fabrics to investigate:

- water repellency
- breathability
- stretch and recovery
- weight
- colour stability
- coatings used
- fibre content.

Being seen

How can cycle-wear be made safer? You can see from the chart that cycle accidents happen by day and night. 'I just didn't see you in time' is what motorists often say after a road accident involving a cyclist.

Fluorescent material works out of doors in the daytime because it reacts to the ultraviolet (UV) rays in sunlight, which make it glare. Fluorescent material really makes you stand out in daylight, but it doesn't work at night.

Reflective material works in the dark because its special surface reflects the light back. It doesn't work in daylight, but if a light shines on it (such as car headlights) it shows up well.

You will need to choose:

- whether to combine fluorescent and reflective materials in your design
- where to put them on your design for the best effect
- whether particular patterns are more effective than others
- fun ways to make your design attractive for the group who will use it.

In designing for manufacture you will need to think early in the design process about:

- the cost of reflective and fluorescent material
- how to use the minimum amount of material for the best effect
- how to keep your design simple to assemble.

To test your design ideas, you could investigate a range of materials using fluorescent lighting tubes, which emit some UV rays. You can investigate the effectiveness of different reflective materials by shining a light on them in a darkened room or cupboard. You must make sure that you use a fair test though.

19

Fit and fun

Case study: Fashion 2000

These students produced some excellent designs for 'Safer Wear for Cyclists' in a competition run by West Nottinghamshire College. The presentation of their work may give you some ideas for your portfolio.

Christopher Glover, Sarah Marsh, Iain Naylor and Roderick Hopkins from Ordsall Hall School.

Case study: Textiles Industry in Partnership with Schools

Kirkby Centre School in Nottinghamshire worked on a design brief which had been set by a local company, Monarch Textiles. Monarch make safety garments in special fabrics which reflect day and night lights, and were looking to move into an additional market area by developing sportswear for teenagers. The students designed new ways for this special fabric to be used in a range of fun and attractive sportswear to be produced commercially. The students went to visit the factory, developed their own patterns, and then cut out and made their own garments. They then showed their designs at a fashion show.

Case study: Douglas Gill – Speed Skins

Douglas Gill designed clothing for the 1996 Great Britain Olympic sailing teams to use in Georgia, where daytime temperatures are 90°F (32.2°C) and the humidity is 90 per cent. Conventional waterproof sailing wear would be totally unsuitable. The design specification required the clothing to:

- help keep sailors cool and comfortable
- protect from sun and ultraviolet light
- be highly breathable
- be aerodynamic
- be wind resistant
- be light-weight.

The designers worked with leading fabric manufacturers and trialled the use of coated fleece and light breathable waterproof fabrics. The most suitable and popular garments with the Olympic team were the heat-reflecting all-white body suits (Speed Skins) and ultraviolet protective smocks. Both these garments fitted the design specification.

UV protective smock:

- 100 per cent nylon, Meryl microfibre
- ultraviolet resistant
- highly breathable
- wind resistance provided by close microfibre weave
- soft to handle.

The smock is long-sleeved for sun protection with a loose, comfortable fit. The soft-lined collar protects the neck from sun. There is a Velcro front opening, a front patch pocket and a drawstring hem.

Speed Skins:

- a laminate of knitted Lycra and hydrophilic film
- breathable, wind and waterproof fabric with omnidirectional stretch
- fine polyester fleece lining laminated to the inside of the suit to increase insulation.

Speed Skins are a stretchy one-piece body-warmer which behave like a very light wetsuit with light thermal properties. On a hot day it is ideal for wearing on its own. The lining is comfortable and does not itch or irritate the skin. In cooler and wetter conditions the suit can be worn as a snug-fitting thermal layer under a drysuit.

What has Douglas Gill learnt from this?
The developments from the Olympic programme will be used in Gill's technical range of dinghy sailing wear. What other sports would benefit from having this type of clothing?

Students from Holgate School and Ashfield School worked with the company Netz Sportswear to develop these new sportswear ranges.

Survival

Your challenge

Life can be comfortable – many of us may never have to survive in a life-threatening situation or environment. However, to test their survival skills, some people choose to put themselves into high risk situations under controlled conditions.

Unfortunately, too many people across the world find themselves in desperate survival situations without any choice. Fortunately, there are many agencies dedicated to supporting people in desperate situations. Well designed and made products can help people survive many dangers, and help those who rescue or assist them.

Your challenge is to identify, research and analyse a survival situation, then to design and make a product that will help people to survive or support anyone helping them.

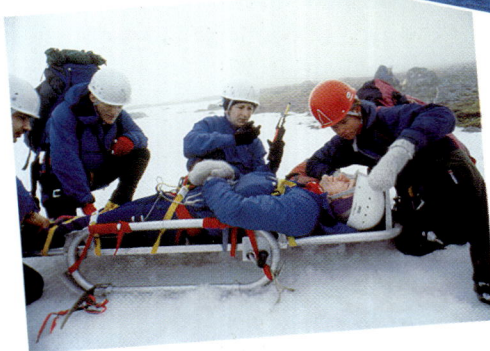

Why this activity is useful

You will have an opportunity to design and make a product that is of great value to the people who will use it. In doing this you will learn to research and understand user needs and constraints in a real way. Someone's life may depend on the product.

You might be able to have your product evaluated in use by experts and may be able to patent your product's design.

You may want to give the idea to an aid agency or emergency service.

Values issues

This designing and making assignment gives you a special opportunity to think more about values. Because surviving often depends on others besides the survivor, it may help you to think about these other points of view as well. In particular:

◆ Should people pay for their rescue if they put themselves in potentially dangerous situations, and then need help?
◆ Should all people be treated in the same way?
◆ How should rescue services be funded?
◆ What do you think about situations where people are starving to death but foreign aid is rejected by their governments?
◆ Should poor countries have to buy essential products when wealthy nations throw the same things away?
◆ Should there be an international force to respond to natural disasters?

To be successful

The real success for you will be the satisfaction of designing and making a product to help another person in some way, possibly in a life-saving way.

★ Choose a risk situation that you can deal with in school even if it needs outside collaboration.
★ Be clear about the amount of risk and the level of trust that will be needed in your product. Avoid situations where the risk or trust involved may turn out to be too great.
★ This will be a piece of your assessed coursework. You can increase your chances of exam success by being clear about what the marking scheme expects from you.

How to get going

The first requirement of this assignment requires some lateral thinking – thinking around the problem.

▶ Two categories of survival situation are given in the project brief – what are they?
▶ Use these two categories to list situations where survival is at stake.
▶ Choose some to analyse carefully for the risks involved and potential products that may reduce those risks. (NB Your syllabus might restrict the type of product that is suitable.)
▶ Do you have any survival experiences to relate your work to?
▶ Can you get close to a real experience of other survival situations you identify?
▶ Can you talk to people with experience of real survival situations?

BEWARE: you will probably need to visit people and places, take photographs, write letters and wait for replies. All of this is time consuming and needs to be included in your planning.

Textiles talk

Textiles can be used as a medium to **convey a message** that people feel strongly about. It could be a political issue like homelessness or blood sports, or an environmental concern such as pollution, destruction of habitats, and so on. Or perhaps there is something close to home that raises strong feelings, such as an activity centre closing or the bus service into town being cut.

Your challenge is to produce a product such as a T-shirt, sweatshirt, quilt or fashion accessory which could carry a message. Wall-hangings are another good approach. Consider opportunities to manufacture your item in high volume to raise funds for your cause.

Why this activity is useful

You will discover how to use textiles to raise public awareness of a key issue of great concern.

It will help you to understand the role of protest groups and charities, and the way they are funded.

You will learn the design factors needed to make a product that is eye-catching, interesting and, if necessary, saleable.

You will explore marketing ideas and high-volume production techniques.

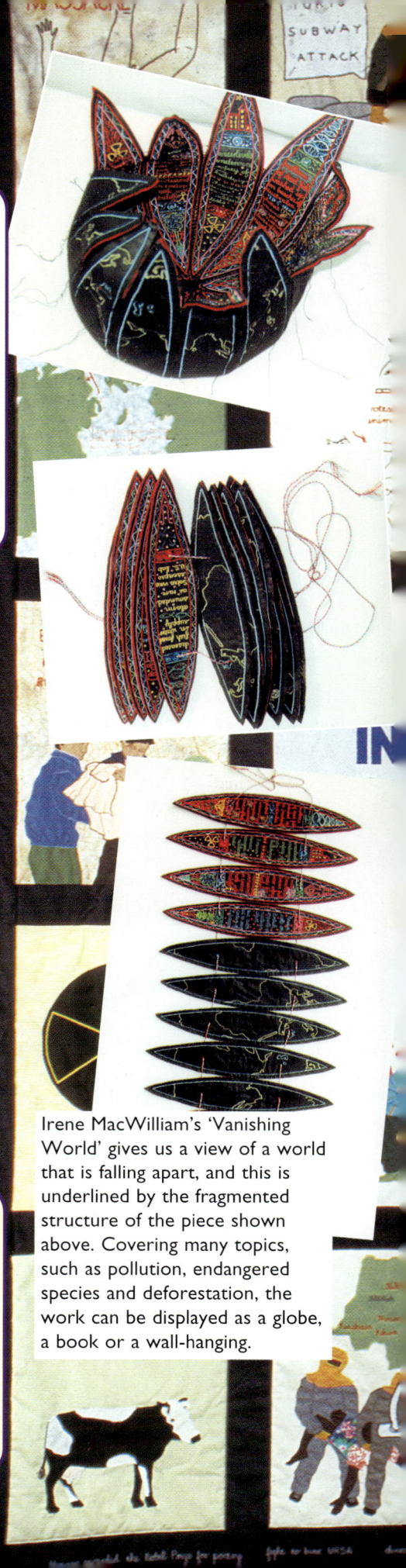

Irene MacWilliam's 'Vanishing World' gives us a view of a world that is falling apart, and this is underlined by the fragmented structure of the piece shown above. Covering many topics, such as pollution, endangered species and deforestation, the work can be displayed as a globe, a book or a wall-hanging.

The design above was created by a community who joined forces to protect the 'smooth spotty snake' whose habitat is threatened by a local building development. The design shown could be stitched on T-shirts, sweatshirts, wallets, caps, and so on, in large quantities.

Values issues

◆ Many of the major charities rely on their product sales to fund the aid they give. How do they sell these products? What do you think are the best items to sell?

◆ Some charities set up 'self-help' projects in poor countries where the people participating can earn money from producing goods. In what ways might this be a better option? Oxfam work with designers to assist in such projects. If you were designing for such a group, what factors would influence you?

◆ We see many examples of violent protest on the TV news. Identify ways in which you could use textile products for a peaceful protest. For example, you could make campaign kites which could be flown at a rally or meeting.

To be successful

Your design and final product will show that you have:

★ researched your theme thoroughly and chosen the most effective means of communication – your aim is to raise awareness of your message, maybe even to shock people into more active concern
★ used your experience to produce strong working designs that will result in a textile product to show off your message in a good, eye-catching way
★ developed a clear idea of the way or ways in which your product will be used in order to make your point.

How to get going

▸ Decide whether the items will be made by individuals or as a classroom project. If necessary, plan a production line for batch production.

▸ Decide on your materials and techniques, and use your working designs to produce samples prior to production. You may scale your designs up or down according to the item being produced. Refer to the manufacturing section of this book for more information.

▸ Analyse your designs and samples. Check consumer reaction. Does the product have the desired effect?

▸ You could use CAD/CAM techniques to create a range of items to be sold to raise funds for your cause.

On the surface

Your challenge

There are many ways to embellish or decorate textiles. You can add **surface decoration** using **appliqué** and **stitching**, you can **dye fabrics** and threads, or you can even create your own fabric or background. By experimenting with different materials you can create some very unusual and exciting effects. Collect together a range of different materials and experiment with ways of putting them together. What effects can you create?

Your challenge is to produce an individual, one-off piece of embellished textiles which would be suitable for a particular purpose, such as a mirror frame, book-cover or bowl. You should include a series of samples showing how you investigated different materials and techniques and developed your final design. Investigate several embellishment techniques before committing yourself.

Why this activity is useful

This project gives you the opportunity to experiment and be creative, trying new techniques and ways of decorating things. You can explore, try out unusual ideas, to create something individual and unique. In doing so you will learn some techniques which you can use in the future when decorating textiles products, and also extend your understanding of the properties and behaviour of materials.

You may also discover new materials to use which will enhance your work in different ways. You can experiment with unconventional materials.

You will become aware of the possibilities available to designer-makers for 'one-off' production.

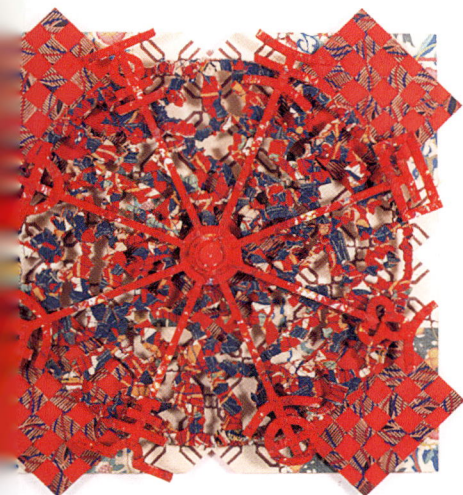

Michael Brennand-Wood uses all kinds of unusual materials in his work (above). 'I believe that all materials have a spirit; it's possible to make most materials do what you want, but it doesn't necessarily feel right. The artist should try to understand what a material is good for and use it accordingly.'

Values issues

◆ 'One-off' manufacture allows for original and unique designs, but has a cost implication. How much would you pay for a cushion that took eight hours to make? How much would a mass-produced cushion cost?

◆ Mass production allows us to benefit from well-designed fabrics and artefacts, but our friends' and neighbours' homes may look very similar to our own. Research ways to customise products by adding decoration.

◆ Manufacture in the Third World may mean that the poorest and youngest people in society work for very low wages to provide beautiful textiles for rich people in the West. How can we stop the exploitation of young people? How can we encourage fair trading? Should we buy products that may have been made in this way?

◆ What does this quote tell us about the way things have changed since the Industrial Revolution?

"There was a time
when each one made a work of art
at the same time as a useful thing
and out of this uniting
burst a spontaneous joy."
William Morris

To be successful

★ Experiment with different techniques and materials.

★ Research and choose a range of suitable materials for colour and texture.

★ Think about different ways of joining fabrics, such as gluing, hand-stitching, machine-stitching and stapling.

★ Consider your final presentation.

How to get going

◗ Collect a range of materials – paper, fabric, leaves, petals and so on. Try changing their appearance using distressing techniques, or by adding paint, stitching or other decoration. Try a range of samples.

◗ Visit your local art gallery or museum and look at how contemporary artists and traditional craftspeople have used materials and techniques in their work.

Technical textiles

Your challenge

Many new textile materials have been developed to meet **special performance requirements**, such as those needed for **survival**, **protection** or for use in **industry**. Designers and technologists continually exploit textile materials to find new and exciting ways of using them. These new products make our lives more interesting and provide more choice for consumers.

Select a flexible material like nylon, plastic or wool and investigate its properties. Is the material thermoplastic? Does it shrink? Find ways of changing the characteristics of your chosen material to develop a new one. Experiment with textile finishing techniques using water or heat.

Your challenge is to develop a new textile and use it to make a product suitable for use through the 21st century. You will need to consider how people's lifestyles will change.

Kevlar has been used for over 15 years to provide light-weight body armour. A new improved version, Kevlar 'Comfort', has been specially engineered for use in ballistic vests that are even lighter and more comfortable.

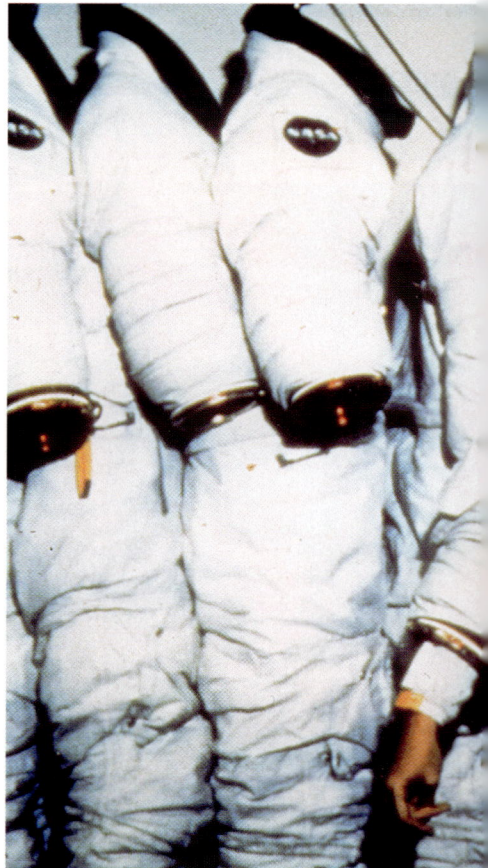

Screen stencils of Trevira monofil fibres can be used to print electronic circuits.

Why this activity is useful

This project will enable you to explore and exploit the properties of flexible materials, and to experiment with textile finishing techniques.

You will be able to use your creative talents to develop a new flexible material or fabric that meets the performance requirements of your intended new product.

You will have the opportunity to learn about the new 'smart' technical fabrics designed to meet special performance requirements.

The assignment is experimental, and you will need to adapt and change your designing and making specifications as the project develops.

You can design and make a product that will add excitement or comfort to the lifestyle of people in the future.

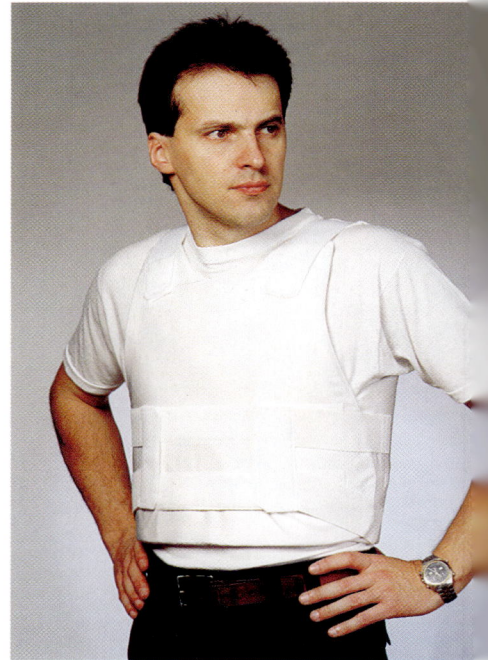

Space shuttle astronauts are protected by clothing made from Nomex III fabric, which protects them from flash fires and doesn't melt.

Values issues

- What will life be like in the future? Will we work at home and only go out to socialise? Who will use interactive technology for their entertainment? What kind of textiles products will we need? Discuss your ideas in groups.
- Will you be designing your new product for function or fun?
- Many textile products are thrown away before they are worn out. How can we encourage people to make use of these waste fabrics?
- Landfill sites are full of plastic bags and bottles which take years to rot down. Plastic bottles can be recycled and made into fibres for use in knitwear or outdoor clothing. In groups, discuss ways to encourage consumers to demand this type of recycling.

To be successful

- ★ Investigate the properties of a range of performance textiles that are used for protection, survival or sport.
- ★ Use your knowledge of the properties of fibres, plastics and finishing techniques to change the way your chosen textile behaves.
- ★ Experiment with ways to develop your new material by stitching or bonding.
- ★ Make a prototype product which can be used for either performance or fun, using your specially-designed new material.
- ★ Put on a display or make a video of your group's new technological products. Invite a local newspaper reporter or a manufacturer to see it.

How to get going

- Make a class collection of performance products for activities such as cycling, in-line skating or swimming. Evaluate and match the performance requirements of each product with the properties of the fabrics used.
- Select and investigate the properties of a flexible material such as nylon, polyester, polypropylene, wool, Vilene or dissolving fabric.
- Experiment with finishing techniques using water or heat to melt or felt your material. Work safely with hot materials and beware of fumes and other hazards.
- Try giving added value to your new fabric by stitching or bonding other materials to it.

TECHNICAL TEXTILES

Crossing cultures

Many new designs are based on traditional garment shapes and themes taken from different cultural backgrounds. Traditional garment shapes, such as the kimono, have been used to develop nightwear designs. Recently, the sarong has been used to develop skirt designs and beachwear.

Different cultural traditions have special pictures, colours and symbols to represent their beliefs and traditions. Often these symbols are used as a basis for developing new pattern designs for fabrics.

Your challenge is to design and make a garment using the influence of a chosen culture. You will have to research carefully and choose whether to retain the authenticity of the original design or use the influence to develop something completely new by combining it with other design influences.

Students from Garibaldi School worked with the Japanese fabric manufacturer 'Toray Textiles' through the Textiles Industry in Partnership with Schools project (TIPS).

Why this activity is useful

You will understand how many designs are developed from traditional sources, and how these designs have been adapted from and combined with those of other cultures.

You will develop an awareness of the meanings behind patterns, symbols and colours.

You will experiment with a range of materials and decorative techniques. You may like to use traditional techniques to retain the authenticity of your design.

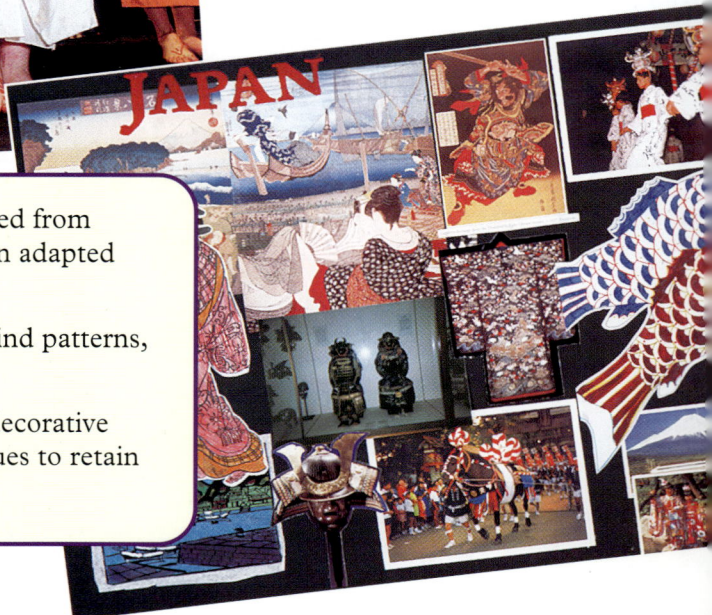

Chosen Design

KIMONO

running stitch.

I'd sew the scales
on the blue fish using
applique.

Values issues

◆ Clothes are used to make personal statements and have to be suited to the lifestyle of the wearers, for example to keep the wearer cool in hot climates, or to keep the body covered where not to do so might be considered offensive. The resources and traditional skills of an area have also influenced garment designs – for example, cotton clothes are produced in cotton-growing areas. Investigate a particular country or area to find out why garments have developed in the way they have.

◆ **Migration** of cultures has meant that the traditional designs from one culture or country have been used to develop new ideas in other cultures. This is often seen in 'East-meets-West' influences in the fashion industry. How do you feel about traditional designs being adapted in this way? Does it devalue the original meaning behind the designs?

To be successful

★ Research your chosen garment, tracing the development of the design.

★ Be able to explain the significance of the colours, symbols and patterns used.

★ Practise techniques for decoration, adopting traditional methods and using those most appropriate to your design.

★ Your item should be designed and made to a high standard. It should be well constructed and finished, and demonstrate an understanding of pattern-cutting, construction and decoration.

How to get going

▸ Identify a traditional garment. Many of these are based on simple shapes which make them easy to construct.

▸ Use books, museums, CD-ROMs and the world-wide web to research and collect information about styles, colours and decoration, including the methods used.

▸ Present research as a moodboard or storyboard, or in a sketch-book. Include information on the meanings of the patterns, symbols and colours used.

▸ Develop ideas from your findings, and produce samples using decorative techniques. Evaluate these outcomes.

▸ Produce paper templates for the pattern pieces, and a prototype of the garment, before constructing and decorating your final design.

Made to order

Your challenge

A manufacturer's production methods vary to suit the items and numbers being made. Some are more adaptable than others, and allow quick response to changes in demand. The industry uses sales information from the shops about which products are selling, then manufactures the right quantity of goods and delivers them as quickly as possible.

Your challenge, as a team, is to set up an **enterprise venture** to design and manufacture a textile product to be sold at your school fair.

Set up a production system which enables fast manufacture of your item, allowing for variety to meet changes in demand (for example, different sizes, colours or decorations). Carry out research to aid designing, make prototypes to test ideas, and check the availability of materials and equipment. Consider the skills needed, costs involved and time allowed.

Why this activity is useful

In this project you will be setting up a production system which emulates the fast production of the textiles industry. Throughout you will learn about production methods that will enable you to respond quickly to your customers' demands. Work as a team and share out the work by breaking down manufacture into systems and sub-systems.

You will practise organising a safe and efficient workspace that will speed up your production time.

You will also discover how important planning and the selection of appropriate equipment and materials are to your success, and how the economic use of these will keep down costs of production.

You will learn about quality control checks at critical points, and use information technology (IT) such as CAD/CAM and spreadsheets.

Values issues

◆ Why should industry conserve the materials it uses, and how might more use be made of recycling outgrown clothing? What issues are raised when you consider the way we use our natural resources, and that we are a throw-away society?

◆ How important is it for industry to balance profit-making with the working environment, production methods and job satisfaction?

◆ In today's working environment the trend is moving away from 'a job for life'. Is this a good or a bad thing?

To be successful

Both the products you make and the whole project will be evaluated. You will have to show that:

★ products meet the desired criteria

★ critical path analysis shows good organisation and time planning

★ flow charts show that manufacture has been planned logically and provision made for feedback loops to check progress

★ attention has been paid to quality assurance and control and critical control points identified

★ the production line is balanced to ensure smooth working and full participation by all team members

★ waste is kept to a minimum by economical lay planning

★ spreadsheets show costings.

How to get going

▶ Working as a team and setting up a production system is not easy! Before you start this project, run a simulation on a simple item that you have made before. Make a batch of the item, working as a team. Record how the activity went and evaluate how you worked together. This will help you develop a clear idea of the difficulties ahead in this challenge.

▶ Identify suitable simple products that are quick to manufacture. Can templates be used to ensure consistency in production? Can you use CAD/CAM? Consider ways of changing the colour, size and decoration. When will this need to take place in your production process?

▶ Make prototypes to check your idea.

▶ Break down production into smaller tasks. Time each stage of manufacture so that the line of production can be balanced and the jobs shared out. Identify critical control points.

DESINGING

What are textiles products?

Originally a **textile** simply meant a woven fabric which could be used for clothes or household goods like bed-linen. These days textiles include an enormous range and variety of innovative products made from many different types of raw materials.

Fibres are the basic components, and are derived from natural or synthetic (manufactured) sources. Fibres are spun into **yarns**, which are then combined using techniques such as weaving or knitting into **textiles**. (The words 'textiles' and '**fabrics**' are sometimes interchanged: the word 'textiles' can refer to a material, cloth or fabric). Exciting developments are taking place at all these three levels, and in the **finishing** of textiles, to bring new opportunities for fashion or technical innovations in **textiles products**.

Textiles are used not only for products such as the clothes and furnishings with which you are familiar, but also for a whole range of technically demanding functions in areas such as the aerospace and automobile industries, agriculture, civil engineering and medicine. Clothing, too, is benefiting from technical developments in 'performance textiles' for special applications.

'Beastly' fashion from UK designer Alexander McQueen, who designs for Givenchy in Paris. His collection included ripped animal skins, goat fur and bleached denim. He is said to 'break all the rules'. What do you think?

Case study: Formula 1 racing

Racing drivers used to wear cotton overalls which were strong, abrasion-resistant and cool to wear. But it meant that they had no protection against flames and heat. Now Formula 1 drivers and car mechanics look like space-age technicians in their colour co-ordinated protective clothing. This is made from Nomex 111 which is a strong, comfortable and heat-resistant textile.

When the Austrian racing driver Gerhard Berger crashed while travelling at around 200 mph during the San Marino Grand Prix in 1996 his car burst into flames. He was saved by the fast action of rescue teams and his protective clothing. Berger's injuries were limited, and he was able to return to racing within a month.

Stop and think

Think about the products that you use every day that are made of textile materials. What would your life be like without them? Textile products provide you with comfort, protection, style, colour and excitement.

What other examples of textile products can you think of?

About a third of all textiles are used in industrial and engineering products. Polyester yarns, fabrics and non-wovens are used for products ranging from sewing threads, ropes and sails to demanding engineering applications. The roof of this stadium in the Munich Olympic Park makes use of high-tenacity polyester fabric.

Savithri Bartlett has researched the thermoplastic properties of two polyester polymers that melt at different temperatures. She has exploited this characteristic to blend polyester with multi-coloured acrylics to create a range of flat and moulded fabrics. This non-woven dome-shaped hat made by Savithri has been used by Karl Lagerfeld of Chanel.

Ruth developed a textile piece inspired by the work of textile artist Louise Baldwin.

35

Where do new ideas come from?

New ideas in textiles develop for a number of reasons, depending on what the product is going to be used for. Textile designers working in different market sectors, such as aerospace, fashion, sportswear or civil engineering, have to take into account many different design factors.

> ▶ **D&T Routes Core Book**
> **pages 44–46**

Factor one: market-place demand

The needs of the market-place or **consumer demand** can influence textile designers and manufacturers. One example is 'easy-care', where consumers demand products which are comfortable and easy to care for. Textile designers and manufacturers have to take note of consumer demands to sell their products, so they must:

◆ be clear about who their customers are
◆ listen to and act upon their demands
◆ find out about their competitors' reaction to market demand, by looking at their products.

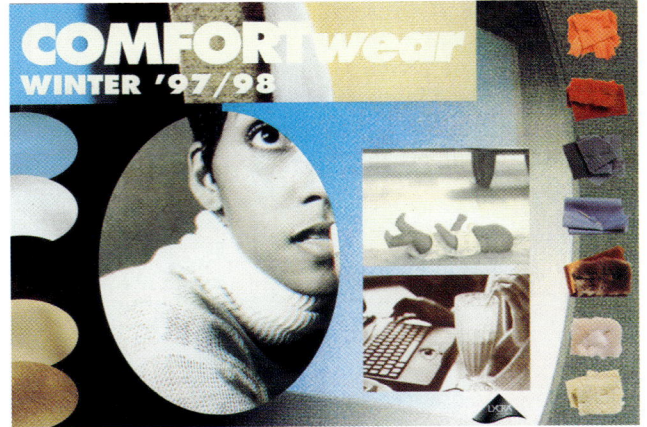

Manufacturers need to take notice of consumers' demands.

Focused task: Products and customers

How do customer demands affect choices when buying leisure clothing? We are all influenced by varying factors, such as designer labels, colour and style or price. Make a list of all the factors that might influence your choice when buying a T-shirt. Do these factors generally match your product choice?

Where do industrial designers get their ideas from? What influences the design of car upholstery, architectural textiles or bouncy castles?

Factor two: new situations

Desire for adventure or different leisure activities can create opportunities for textile development to meet new challenges. For example, the need to protect people who work in dangerous situations means thinking mainly about safety issues and function rather than aesthetics. The main criteria for many textile products such as tyres, protective clothing or geotextiles is their function, strength and fitness for purpose.

New situations can lead to new ideas for textile fibres and fabrics and for textile processes like finishing. This has resulted in:

◆ new fibres like Tencel and microfibres of nylon or polyester
◆ 'smart' microfibre fabrics with improved properties and handle
◆ performance textiles which are 'breathable'
◆ new uses of technical textiles for architecture or geotextiles
◆ new treatments like anti-bacterial finishes for medical textiles
◆ unforeseen benefits, like Teflon-coated fabrics that are wind, water or stain-resistant.

The excitement and glamour surrounding sport often hides the danger to life and limb. New sports like in-line skating require specialist equipment for protection at every joint.

Factor three: redesigning to add value

Textiles products are continually redesigned to improve their performance, function or appeal. Styles change to keep consumers interested in buying new products. Advertising campaigns often promote new fibres, fabrics, easy-care finishes and 'designer labels'.

Exciting innovations in textile technology, such as Lycra, have led to the redesign of many sportswear products.

Stop and think

It is expensive to replace curtains or upholstered furniture, so retailers like Habitat or Ikea need to create consumer demand. This is often done by 'lifestyle marketing', which means promoting styles that meet their target customers expectations.

● Look for advertisements that promote lifestyle.
● Identify the target consumer group and design style being promoted.

Factor four: social and cultural influences

Designers need to be aware of social trends evident in the latest news story, exhibition or film. Recent interest in fitness has led to the 1990s being called the 'decade of the body', with many designers producing their own sportswear-inspired clothing. Designers also look to other cultures or artists to inspire their work.

Do the right thing!

● Decide who you are designing for, and research their needs and preferences.
● Analyse existing high-performance textiles or new materials for possible use by you.
● Collect images that interest or inspire you.
● Review the latest films to spot trends and influences.
● Go to exhibitions and museums.
● Investigate textiles from other cultures.
● Try redesigning an existing textile for a different end use or user.
● Try using existing materials in a new context.
● Explore ways to use recycled materials.

Generating ideas

How do textiles product designers work?

The manufacturing process for any textile product begins with the designer. Some textiles designers create clothing for the mass market for high street shops while others design products for more functional end-uses, like Welbeck geotextiles (see page 92). All designers must be creative and have a good technical knowledge, so that their ideas can be translated into saleable products.

Focused task: Designers at work

Do designers of products that are primarily functional work in the same way as designers of fashion products? Use the designing information below to help discuss the differences.

Designers who work in the clothing, accessories and interiors market sector need to:

◆ be aware of current and future colour and style trends
◆ understand consumer needs, keeping up to date with films, music and other areas of art and design
◆ be aware of moral, cultural, environmental and social issues that influence textile design
◆ keep up to date with technical information and materials
◆ know what textile products are on the market
◆ understand the limitations caused by working to budget.

Designers who work with more functional products need to:

◆ keep up to date with technical information and materials
◆ know what products are on the market
◆ understand the limitations caused by working to budget
◆ understand client company needs.

Starting points for your designing

Working to a theme can enable you to develop ideas which may be incorporated into new product designs. Sometimes the brief can give you a theme which needs to be in sympathy with the product or

Functional Requirements for Permanent Architectural Fabrics	
Tensile strength	227 k/25 mm for air-supported structures 295 k/25 mm for pre-tensioned structures
Durability	functional for at least 20 years
Fire safety	meets existing building regulations
Energy efficiency	adequate daylight without artificial light acceptable levels of heat gain/loss
Cost	life-cycle cost competitive with conventional architecture
Aesthetics	an exciting structural alternative to traditional architecture

Using moodboards

Moodboards are used by designers to show clients their ideas for new products. The moodboard communicates ideas on design, illustrating themes, styling details, shapes, colours, texture, pattern and fabrics.

This student designed a moodboard using a tartan influence.

D&T Challenges Blue Book
Moodboards, page 42

the target market. For example, the theme for an active leisurewear look for children could be 'punk', and focus on modern city styles using bright 'electric' colours.

Looking at existing products

Textile designers often take apart (or **disassemble**) textiles products when they want to develop new ideas. This provides a useful checklist for developing a specification for a new product, and can be useful in analysing a competitor's product.

▶ **D&T Routes Core Book**
pages 26–42

It is easier to develop design ideas for real-life situations and known people. How is the textile product going to be used? Where will it be used? Who will use it? What are their likes and dislikes?

Before you begin your design research, decide on the things you need to know. This student visited a garden centre to research the kinds of products sold there. The chart was useful for recording what she saw.

Textile Products at the Garden Centre

	function	target market	cost	fabric	properties	manufacture	fastening	aftercare
Waistcoat	keeps you warm	male/ female over 35	£10-20	poly/ cotton wadding from polyester	warm easy-fit	quilted mass-produced	zip	machine-wash drip-dry
Sun-hat	protects from sun	child under 5	under £5	100% cotton			adjustable popper	
Shopping bag	carrying things	female over 25	£5-10	coated cotton				

You could research a textile product and produce a chart similar to this one.

▶ **D&T Routes Core Book**
Using your research, page 90

Case study: Disassembly

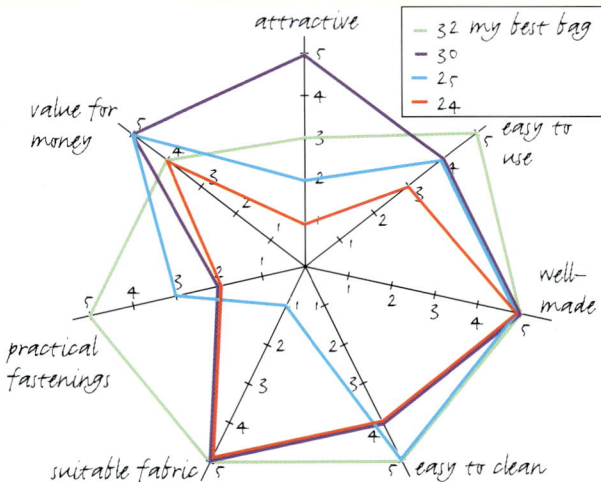

This student found her best bag using a star diagram.

Some students made a collection of used bags. Each student evaluated a range of bags to find which one was the best. They used the following questions as a guide.

- What is the bag used for, and who would use it?
- Is it easy to use and practical?
- Is it well made from suitable materials and fastenings?
- Does the bag have any special features?
- Is the bag attractive and good value for money?
- Can it be improved?

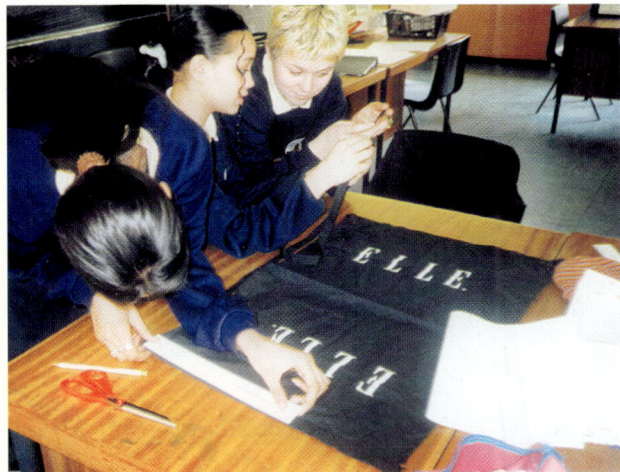

Each student then had to:

- sketch their best bag design
- carefully take it apart
- sketch all the sections of the bag, making a note of how they fitted together.

The results of the disassembly and evaluation exercise enabled each student to develop a design specification for a new bag.

Look at a similar product to the one you are going to design, and take it apart to find out how it is made. Use the case study to help you.

Generating ideas

In the style of...

The work of other designers and artists has always been used as a starting point for design work. It is part of design development to build on what has gone before. Visit an exhibition or art gallery to see how other designers have found solutions to design problems.

Keep an ideas book when you visit an exhibition. Make sketches of the work that you like and keep a note of techniques used. Look at the way the work is presented and if possible include photos and postcards. Explain why you like the work. Then try the exercise on page 57 of the *D&T Routes Core Book* to get you going.

Case study: Visiting exhibitions

A group of students visited an exhibition in Nottingham to look at the work of six textile artists. They were very impressed by the designs of Louise Baldwin, who works creatively with a range of textile materials, paper and nails. The students used elements of what they had seen in their own work.

A student's sketch of the work of textile artist Louise Baldwin.

Inspired by ... other cultures

As a designer you need to have a store of images that you can use to help you find design ideas. You could collect pictures of clothing and artefacts worn or used in other cultures. Keep a scrap-book of things that interest you for whatever reason – it could be for colour or pattern, or simply that you like it! This will help your research and give you ideas.

Case study: The Masai of Africa

The way the Masai from East Africa adorn their bodies with intricate beaded jewellery has changed little since the 19th century. In recent spring/summer collections the UK designer John Galliano and the American designer Ralph Lauren used the influence of the Masai in their own designs.

Textiles student Martha Slipp also used inspiration from African tribal designs to help develop her work. She researched and studied Masai decorative beaded jewellery, sketching it and experimenting with techniques. Martha's 'Neckpiece' was made using hand-made paper with leaves, appliqué and machine embroidery.

Masai-inspired design on the catwalk.

A student made this piece of textile body adornment based on studies of Masai head-dresses and collars.

Experimenting with ideas

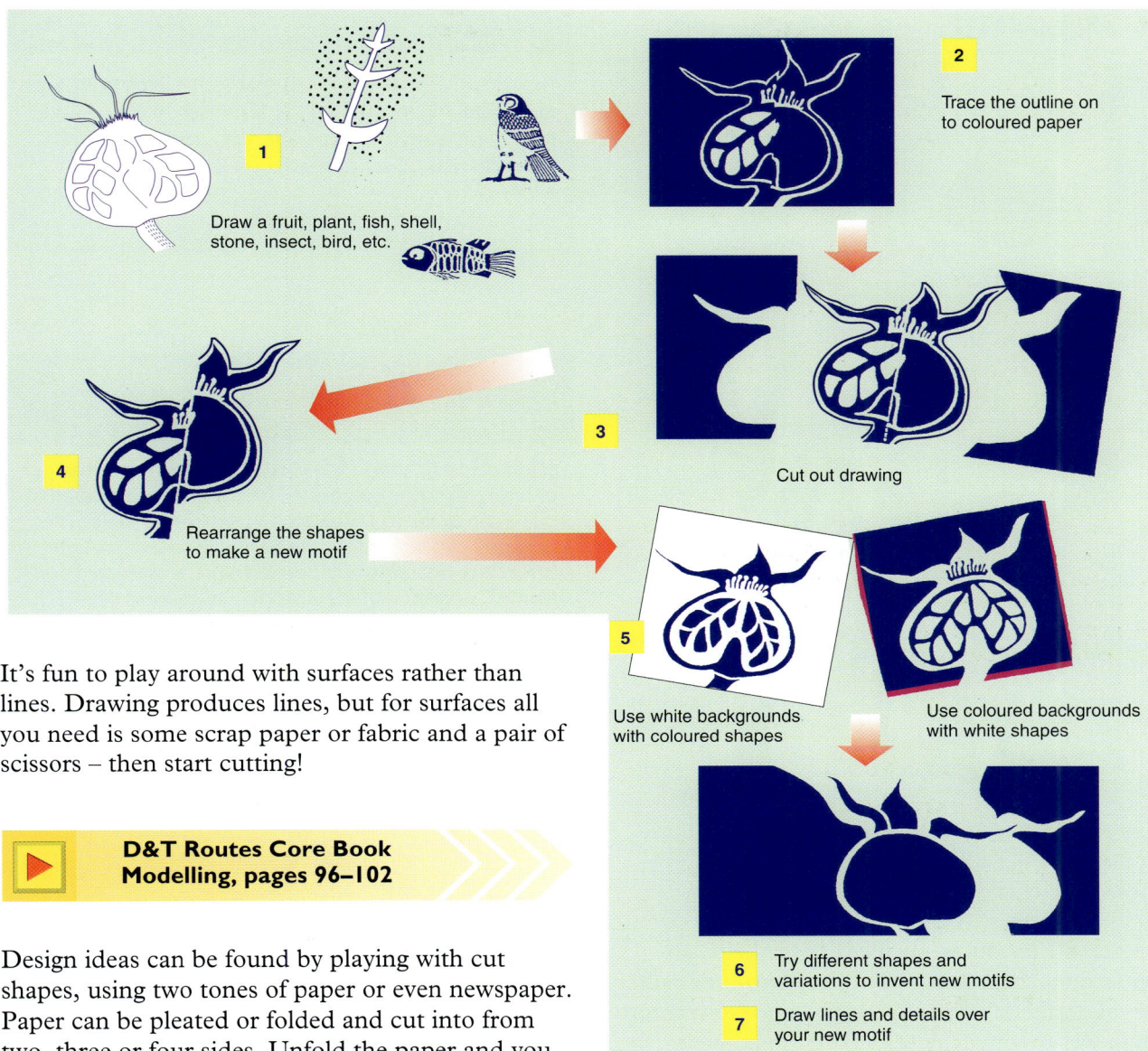

1 Draw a fruit, plant, fish, shell, stone, insect, bird, etc.

2 Trace the outline on to coloured paper

3 Cut out drawing

4 Rearrange the shapes to make a new motif

5 Use white backgrounds with coloured shapes

Use coloured backgrounds with white shapes

6 Try different shapes and variations to invent new motifs

7 Draw lines and details over your new motif

It's fun to play around with surfaces rather than lines. Drawing produces lines, but for surfaces all you need is some scrap paper or fabric and a pair of scissors – then start cutting!

▶ **D&T Routes Core Book**
Modelling, pages 96–102

Design ideas can be found by playing with cut shapes, using two tones of paper or even newspaper. Paper can be pleated or folded and cut into from two, three or four sides. Unfold the paper and you have a design of regularly-repeated pattern formations. If you want to change the pattern, just refold the paper and cut out more. The scraps that were cut out can be used to make a new pattern idea.

◆ Draw over your pattern with coloured pencils or trace over it and add colour.
◆ Scan your design into a computer and copy, rotate or mirror image it.

New ideas can be developed by weaving strips from cut or torn coloured paper, magazines, newspaper, gift-wrap or brown paper. Weave straight or askew, close together or far apart. Your weave ideas can be traced and re-coloured to develop a new design.

Designers adapt and simplify drawn shapes and colours to get 'motifs' they can use for their work.

This bag by Louise Baldwin is made from recycled juice cartons.

Thinking about ...

Function when designing

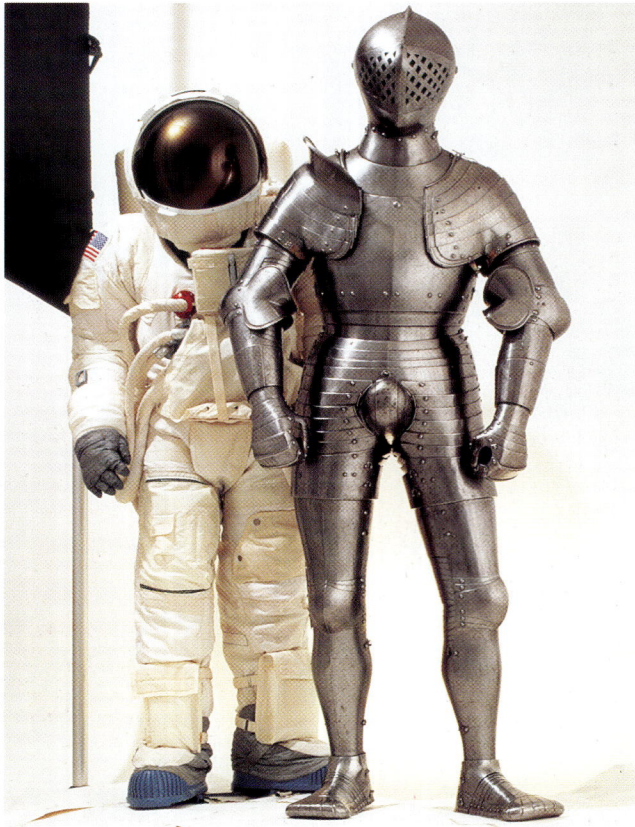

Compare the body armour of Henry VIII with the space suit. The purpose of each is the survival of its wearer.

Many textile products, such as car seatbelts, are produced for their **functional performance** rather than for aesthetic values like appearance or comfort. Denim was originally developed as functional workwear because of its hard-wearing properties, before it became street fashion for generations of people. Today's outdoor pursuits wear is designed using colours and fabrics that support the fashion 'look', but the major function is performance. This depends on fibres and fibre engineering.

All textiles products need to be designed with a **function** or end-use in mind, to help produce a quality product that people really need. Think how you could design a textile product without taking into account its function!

D&T Routes Core Book page 66

Focused task: Functions of textile products

Functional textile products make our lives safer and more fun. Make a list of the activities that you take part in on a regular basis and the textile products that you use. Specify what you require one textile product to do, evaluate its existing properties, and explain how it could be improved.

Case study: Ballooning around the world

Attempts to fly round the world non-stop led to the use of high-tech textile materials, which were developed to make the Breitling (1) balloon as safe as possible. The balloon's gas cell was made from laminated gas-tight nylon, the heat-resistant balloon 'skirt' was made from Nomex, and the outer envelope was made from aluminised Mylar to reduce heat loss at night and minimise solar heating during the day.

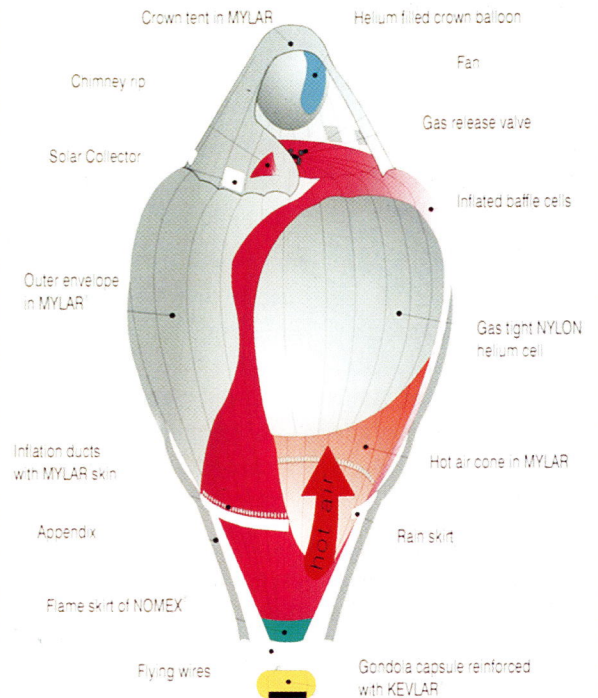

Attempts to fly non-stop round the world made use of high-tech functional textile materials.

Thinking about ...

Style and colour when designing

Architect Ron Heron designed the headquarters of the design consultancy Imagination Ltd. The narrow space between two buildings was roofed with PVC-coated polyester fabric to form a light and exciting space, combining function with beauty.

You are expected to design and make textile products that fulfil aesthetic criteria such as being attractive, colourful or stylish. Designers often have to work toward a particular style, perhaps to suit a certain market (such as formal, leisure or business).

▶ **D&T Routes Core Book**
Style, page 73

Case study: Defining style

A student was asked to say what was meant by style. He said that style is:

- all to do with the way things look
- to be totally confident about your appearance
- something that others admire
- the 'in thing' – a fashion statement
- something that comes naturally.

These students from Sconce Hills School designed stylish leisurewear for young people and presented their designs at a fashion show.

Focused task: What is style?

Think about the following questions.

- What do you think style is?
- Does it mean different things to different people?
- Who do you think has style?
- Could you describe their style in a word or two?

Focused task: Style through colour

Brightly coloured textiles are the fashionable style for clothes and interiors from time to time. Different colour combinations can change the style of an interior, evoking the feeling of different moods or another era. Think about your colour choices for a moodboard with the style theme 'Tropical'.

The French painter Matisse used clear bright shades of citrus yellow, turquoise and lime green in his paintings. Choose a brightly-coloured painting that you like, take three or four colours from it, and use them as a colour theme in your next textile piece.

Thinking about ...

Cost and prices when designing

D&T Routes Core Book page 74

An accurate costing is needed to calculate the right price to make your textile product saleable and create a profit. Your costing needs to include all the materials used, labour charges and overhead costs such as heating or rent. To this is added the profit to arrive at a price which must also reflect your product's value to your customer.

Is the product a hand-crafted individual design or a low unit cost, mass-produced item? For the product to sell at an affordable price it must be easy to manufacture and well designed, taking into account the available equipment and manufacturing processes.

Stop and think

The fabric used by a manufacturer to make a shirt could represent about 50 per cent of the total cost of production. Using a less expensive fabric would make a real difference to the selling price of the shirt.

Can you cut your cost of production by simplifying your design details or using less expensive materials?

Case study: Cutting costs

	Design details	Production cost for design details		
		cost	labour	total cost
final design	• hand-embroidered logo × 2 hrs @ £3 per hour		6.00	6.00
	• bind pocket edges with bias-binding @ £1 per metre × 50 cm	0.50	1.50	2.00
	• fabric @ £5.99 per metre × 1.50 m	8.99		8.99
				16.99
modified design	• machine embroidered logo × 1 hr @ £3 per hour		3.00	3.00
	• no pocket binding			
	• fabric @ £3.99 per metre × 1.25 m (Smaller seam allowance, new lay plan so less fabric used)	4.99		4.99
				7.99

Students from Quarrydale School worked with clothing manufacturers Coats Viyella to design and make a range of leisurewear. They designed shorts and tops, with each student making up one garment in the range. This student found that her production costs were too high, so she modified her design.

The roof of the Medinah Mosque is made from six huge retractable umbrellas, each nearly 20 metres across. The special fabric was woven from high strength PTFE fibres and the roof was designed to be cost-effective: the minimum amount of fabric and the smallest number of components were used in the construction.

DESIGNING

Thinking about ...

Health and safety when designing

When you design textile products you need to consider the risks that are involved in making and using them. Think about the materials and processes needed to make your product, from the raw materials, through manufacture, to use and disposal. The student below started to draw up a chart about designing a safe textile product. You could use a similar chart when designing yours.

Safety issues – designing/making elbow protection	
Raw materials	safe source, non-toxic, soft
Components	no detachable parts, no sharp edges
Manufacturing processes	clean, safe, minimum chemicals,
Use	comfortable, easy fastenings
Aftercare	easy care, information label
Disposal	clean and safe, biodegradable, recyclable

Many textile products are worn or used next to the skin. Think about the fabric properties needed for underwear, and for in-line skating knee-guards. Many textiles need to be highly visible, or must protect the wearer from impact. You could list the safety requirements for ice-hockey goalkeepers' clothing.

Ice-hockey goalkeepers may suffer many impacts from the ball during a match.

▶ **D&T Routes Core Book pages 84–85**

Case study: Protective equipment

Nearly all activities carry an element of risk. This can be reduced by using **personal protective equipment** (PPE) which is designed to protect against safety or health hazards in activities like high-risk sports or in the workplace. All safety clothing or equipment that is marketed in Europe has to meet specific performance and quality requirements so that it can carry the European Standard 'CE' symbol. It is illegal to attempt to sell any item of PPE without the CE mark. There are three categories of protection.

Maximum protection includes 'complex designs' for protection against mortal danger or serious health hazards. Examples are:

- breathing apparatus which uses carbon fibre
- mountaineering or sailing harnesses which prevent falling or drowning

- chainsaw clothing that protects against serious wounds.

Minimum protection includes 'simple designs' where manufacturers assume that users can assess the level of protection against minimal risks. Examples are:

- gardening gloves
- seasonal clothing.

Intermediate protection includes all other products that are not simple or complex. Examples are:

- lifejackets
- high-visibility clothing
- eye and ear protection.

Thinking about ...

The environment when designing

Designers are becoming more aware of designing with the environment in mind. You can help by using renewable raw materials, cutting down on waste, and reusing or recycling where possible. Modern designers are helping the environment by reusing a variety of unusual materials, such as frozen food packaging, bicycle inner tubes, and even making tea-bag fabrics!

▶ **D&T Routes Core Book**
Product life, page 88

Working with reclaimed materials, Wendy Thomas and Simon Doughty produced cabinets made from driftwood with inlays of hand-made felt. The felt is enhanced by the recycled wood, because one is hard and the other soft.

Focused task: New uses for old

Collect together 'waste' products such as used fabrics, frozen food bags, foil, plastic bags, polythene, nylon and paper. You could try:

- ■ layering and stitching some of these together using a variety of threads
- ■ laminating them between self-adhesive plastic book-covering film
- ■ weaving or knitting strips of fabric to produce varying textures
- ■ testing them for strength and fitness for purpose as a textile material.

Biostoning

Manufacturers are developing new textile processes like dyeing or finishing that are less harmful to the environment. For example, stone-washed denim jeans were traditionally washed with pumice stones but now manufacturers can use enzymes to 'biostone' denim. This eliminates polluted water, causes less machine damage and saves the time and labour costs of removing dust and stones from finished garments.

Eco-labelling

An eco-label on a T-shirt shows that its manufacture has been judged to cause as little environmental damage as possible. The Eco-Labelling Scheme uses a cradle-to-grave approach (dealing with every process and stage the product goes through) to help consumers make choices that reduce the damage being done to the environment. For example, it asks:

- ◆ do the fibres come from a renewable source?
- ◆ how much energy is used to manufacture the fibres, yarns, fabrics and end product?
- ◆ does the manufacture cause pollution to air, water or land?
- ◆ how much energy is used to maintain the textile during its life?
- ◆ what will be the result of disposing of the textile?

Thinking about ...

Product life when designing

When you design a textile product you need to think about its maintenance and how long it will last. Your specification needs to take into account the properties of the materials and components as well as the textile aftercare. Properties such as stretch, strength and durability can affect a textile's fitness for purpose and the product lifespan, and could affect its safety. Think about these properties the next time you fasten your seatbelt!

▶ **D&T Routes Core Book page 86**

Remember follow the care instructions

Washing

Cotton Wash (No bar)		A wash tub without a bar indicates that normal (maximum) washing conditions may be used at the appropriate temperature.
Synthetics Wash (Single Bar)		A single bar beneath the wash tub indicates reduced (medium) washing conditions at the appropriate temperature.
Wool Wash (Broken Bar)		A broken bar beneath the wash tub indicates much reduced (minimum) washing conditions, and is designed specifically for machine washable wool products.
Hand Wash Only		Do not machine wash.

The number in the wash tub shows the most effective wash temperature.

Bleaching

△ Chlorine bleach may be used

Ironing

Hot Iron - Cotton, Linen, Viscose
Warm Iron - Polyester mixtures, Wool
Cool Iron - Acrylic, Nylon, Polyester

Dry Cleaning

Ⓟ May be dry cleaned. Other letters and/or a bar beneath the circle will indicate the required process to the dry cleaner.

Tumble Drying

May be tumble dried:
with high heat setting
with low heat setting
✕ A cross through any symbol means 'DO NOT'

This leaflet has been produced by the Home Laundering Consultative Council (HLCC), the UK textile aftercare and care labelling authority.

HLCC, 5 Portland Place, London W1N 3AA

Ropes made of Kevlar have been used for the stay cables of a footbridge over the River Tay in Scotland.

It's no fun when your favourite sweater is ruined in the wash. A simple way to avoid this is to follow the care instructions on the label.

The life expectancy of a textile item can depend on its end use. Would you expect a pair of jeans to last for ten years? The answer is definitely no – you may change shape or the jeans might wear out. When you design you need to decide on the product life so you can choose an appropriate fabric type. Some textiles can last a long time. Examples of this are linen fabrics found in Egyptian tombs or ancient textiles from South America. Today's technical textiles are often used for their strength and long-life capabilities. Kevlar, a synthetic 'aramid' fibre, is five times stronger than steel and can be used for the stay cables of bridges, for tyres and for reinforcing the hulls of boats. These products definitely need to last as long as possible.

Maintenance

Sometimes the life of a textile product can be extended through good maintenance. For example, motorcycle gloves can be re-waterproofed with a special wax or spray.

Focused task: Looking at labels

Manufacturers of textile clothing or furnishings are legally required to sew in care labels that explain the textile aftercare. Look at the labels on a range of textile products to find out the aftercare needs of different fibres and fibre blends.

Thinking about ...

Materials when designing

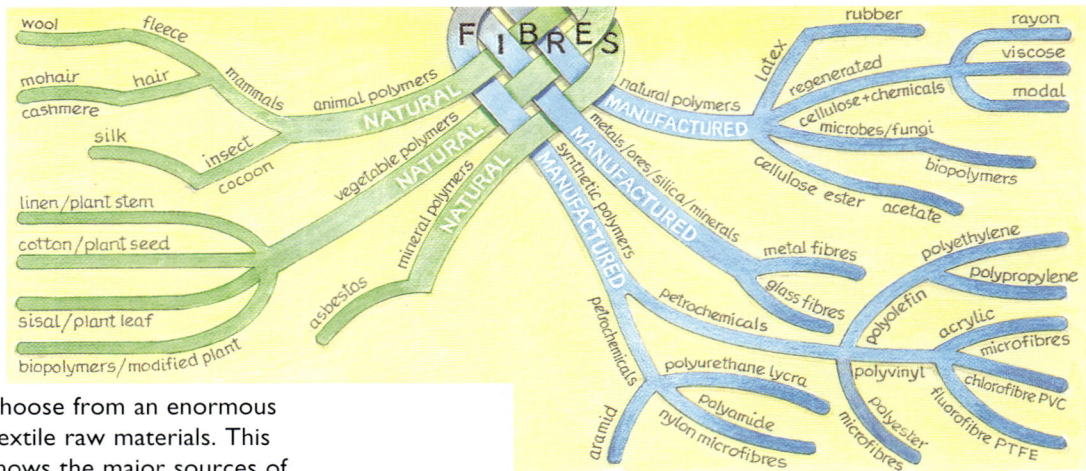

You can choose from an enormous range of textile raw materials. This diagram shows the major sources of natural and manufactured fibres.

You can choose from a wide range of textile raw materials, not just conventional fibres and yarns. Almost any flexible material can be used if it is suitable for your end product. New fibres and fabrics are constantly being developed, so it is helpful to look at product labels to keep up to date.

Looking at fibres

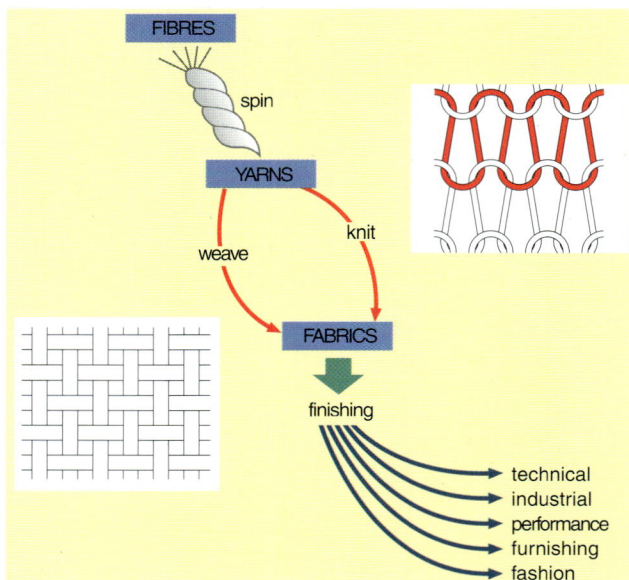

All fibre types have different properties which make them suitable for a variety of uses. Spinning fibres into yarns and then weaving or knitting the yarns into textiles can affect these properties, although fibre and textile properties are very closely linked.

The raw materials of most textile fibres are natural or synthetic polymers. Natural fibres include wool, cotton, linen and silk. Some natural polymers can be 'regenerated' with chemicals to make fibres like rayon, viscose or modal. Synthetic polymers are manufactured to make fibres such as polyester, acrylic and nylon (polyamide).

Fibres can be short or very long depending on where they come from or how they are made.

◆ 'Staple' fibres vary in length from a few millimetres to a metre long. Natural staple fibres include cotton, linen, wool or mohair.
◆ Synthetic fibres are first manufactured as continuous filaments. The fibres can then be cut into staple (or standard) lengths.
◆ Silk is the only natural continuous filament fibre which can be as long as a kilometre.

New fibres

Modern manufactured fibres are used to make a new generation of hard-working, good-looking, comfortable fabrics. Many new fibres are revolutionising the fabrics used for active sportswear, shoes, fashion wear and all-weather wear.

Other new fibres like Lyocell are being used for a range of textile end uses such as:

◆ technical textiles like tent fabrics
◆ non-wovens like medical dressings
◆ special papers like tea-bags.

The synthetic polymer nylon 6.6 is used to make a range of Tactel yarns.

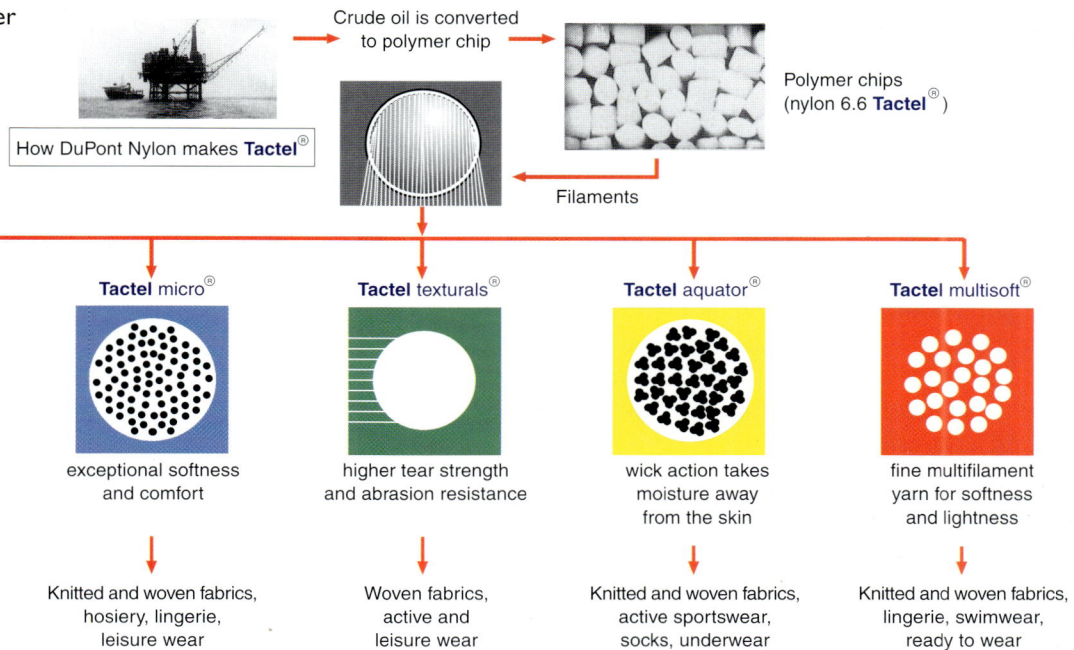

Crude oil is converted to polymer chip

How DuPont Nylon makes **Tactel**®

Polymer chips (nylon 6.6 **Tactel**®)

Filaments

Tactel diabolo®	**Tactel** micro®	**Tactel** texturals®	**Tactel** aquator®	**Tactel** multisoft®
new lustre and drape effects	exceptional softness and comfort	higher tear strength and abrasion resistance	wick action takes moisture away from the skin	fine multifilament yarn for softness and lightness
Knitted and woven fabrics, lingerie, hosiery, ready to wear	Knitted and woven fabrics, hosiery, lingerie, leisure wear	Woven fabrics, active and leisure wear	Knitted and woven fabrics, active sportswear, socks, underwear	Knitted and woven fabrics, lingerie, swimwear, ready to wear

Focused task: Fibres survey

- Look in stores such as Marks & Spencer at new micro-fibres which are strong, smooth, soft and 'drape' well. These fibres are 60 times finer than a human hair!
- See what you can find out about Supplex, Sympatex, Lycra, Tencel, Coolmax, Tactel and Teflon, and make a chart to show their properties and end uses.
- Find examples of fibre blends of natural or synthetic fibres with Lycra that give added comfort and fit.

Focused task: Disassembling yarns

- Cut two different yarns to the same length and count the number of twists in each. Feel the yarns and explain why one is softer than the other.
- Untwist both yarns to see their structure. The yarn could be one single strand or be plied from two or more single yarns. Explain why yarns are plied.
- Untwist the yarns until you are left with the smallest fibre. Measure it to see if it is a staple fibre – or is it a continuous filament?
- Look at your yarn through a microscope to see if it is made from blended fibres. Do the fibres look the same or is one more shiny, fibrous or scaly?

Looking at yarns

Making yarns is highly-skilled work. The thickness of yarn (**yarn count**) and the **yarn twist** affect fabric weight, flexibility, handle and its end-use. Too much twist can make a yarn hard and slow down production, and too little twist results in weak yarn. Soft yarns for knitting usually have less twist, so they are unsuitable for weaving which needs strong yarns.

Yarns can be spun in a clockwise (Z) or anti-clockwise (S) direction of twist, which can produce special effects in fabric. Single yarns can be plied to make strong two-ply or three-ply yarns. Different coloured single yarns can be plied to make 'fancy' yarns. Different fibres can be spun together to make blended yarns like wool/acrylic.

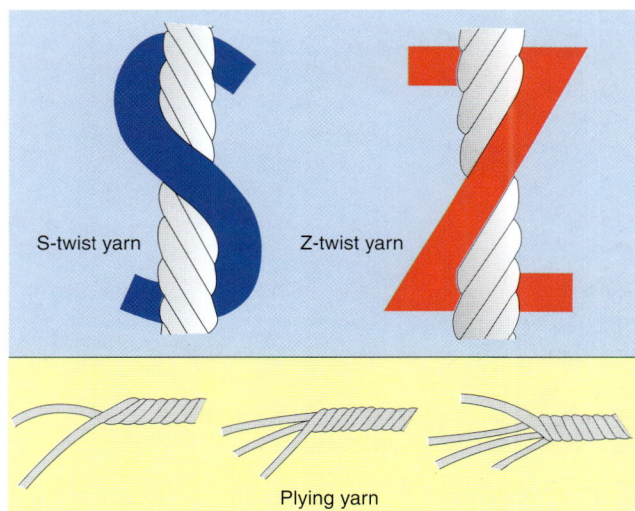

S-twist yarn

Z-twist yarn

Plying yarn

Looking at fabrics

Most manufactured fabrics are woven or knitted, but others are non-woven (such as felt or a J-cloth), braided, lace or crochet. The structure of the fabric will affect not just what it looks like but the way it behaves and feels. For example, knitted fabrics are usually stretchy because they are made from continuous yarn which is looped together. Try stretching your jumper – which direction has the most stretch? Woven fabrics are usually stronger with less stretch, because they are made from yarns which are under tension during manufacture. Try pulling a tea-towel very hard to see if it stretches. Sometimes woven fabrics are made to stretch by using a special fibre blend in the yarn. Which manufactured fibre is stretchy?

▶ **The business of manufacturing page 91**

▶ **In the mood, page 4**

You can find out how textiles are constructed by taking them apart.

Fabric finishing

Fabrics that come straight from the loom or knitting machine need to be finished by a physical or chemical process to make them useful. Finishing is a quality assurance process that makes sure the fabric is free from faults, clean, pre-shrunk and stable.

Careful finishing can improve the appearance, handle and quality of a fabric. Finishes can be:

◆ aesthetic – for appearance or handle
◆ functional – for performance characteristics like 'breathability'
◆ permanent – like dyeing or Durable Press
◆ semi-durable – lasting several launderings, like shower-resistant fabrics
◆ temporary, like pressing – removed by laundering.

Finishing processes			
Physical mechanical processes using heat, steam, pressure, etc.		**Chemical** processes using chemicals that can cause environmental damage	
Brushing	brushed cotton **use**: soft, fleecy, warm nightwear	Anti-bacterial	synthetic fabrics; slows down the growth of bacteria **use**: hospital uniforms
Calendering	glazed cotton **use**: smooth, glossy upholstery fabrics	Fire-resist	cotton (Proban); protects from burns **use**: children's nightwear
Durable press	polyester (thermoplastic) **use**: permanent creases in trousers	Mercerising	cotton, linen; shiny, strong, dyes well **uses**: curtains, clothing
Stone-washing	denim **use**: faded-look jeans	Bio-stoning	denim; natural enzymes make the process more environmentally friendly **use**: faded-look jeans

Safety note!

⚠
◆ Take care when handling hot liquids or equipment.
◆ Wear gloves when handling hot materials, or grip with tongs.
◆ Wear safety goggles where appropriate.
◆ Put material giving off fumes in a well-ventilated area, fume hood or spray booth.
◆ Clean up spills quickly and thoroughly.

Focused task: Fabric finishing techniques

You can use some industrial-type processes to enhance or change your own textiles. Some or all of the following materials may be used for experiments, depending on the effect required:

- wool
- nylon
- polyester
- Vilene
- polyester/cotton
- frozen food bags
- polypropylene
- polythene.

You can exploit the properties of textiles by shrinking, melting or felting using physical processes like:

- washing in hot water and detergent
- boiling in a saucepan
- scrubbing with pan scourers
- ironing between aluminium foil
- brushing with wire brushes
- applying dry heat from a hairdryer or oven.

The new Challenge of Materials Gallery at London's Science Museum aims to show what materials are and how they are selected, made and recycled. This wacky footwear is made from Astroturf by Lucia Simon of Cordwainer's College.

Case study: Stiffening fibres and textiles by heat

Polypropylene (PP) is a fibre that is being used experimentally by young fashion and textile designers. PP is often used for fruit or onion nets, and for sports bag straps. It goes soft at 144°C and melts at 165°C, then loses its softness to become more rigid when left to cool. This change can be used as a design feature for creative work in two or three dimensions.

Textile artist Frances Geesin has used polypropylene in her experimental work. This technique needs release papers such as Teflon (used for lining baking trays) or greaseproof paper.

- Arrange some polypropylene fibres or netting on to a release paper.
- Put a layer of release paper on top and apply a hot iron slowly over the fibres.
- When the paper has cooled, peel it away to find a firm pattern of plastic.

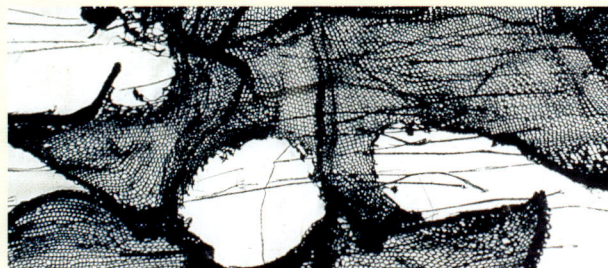

Frances Geesin's 'Black Ice' is made from knitted polypropylene, which was heated by ironing and then cut and fused on to cotton calico.

Textile properties

You can monitor a textile's behaviour when you experiment with finishing processes. Look out for and record the following properties:

- absorbency
- insulation
- stain resistance
- washability
- wear resistance (abrasion)
- strength
- stretch.

Textiles for cycling

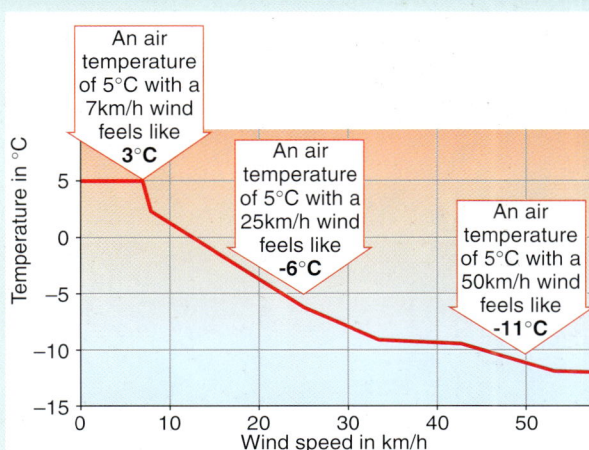

An air temperature of 5°C with a 7km/h wind feels like **3°C**

An air temperature of 5°C with a 25km/h wind feels like **-6°C**

An air temperature of 5°C with a 50km/h wind feels like **-11°C**

Textiles for cycling need to be wind-resistant to maintain the warming micro-climate between the skin and the garment. Cycling downhill at 30 mph in a temperature of 5°C would feel like it was minus 11°C outside.

Thinking about materials when designing

SealSkinz gloves

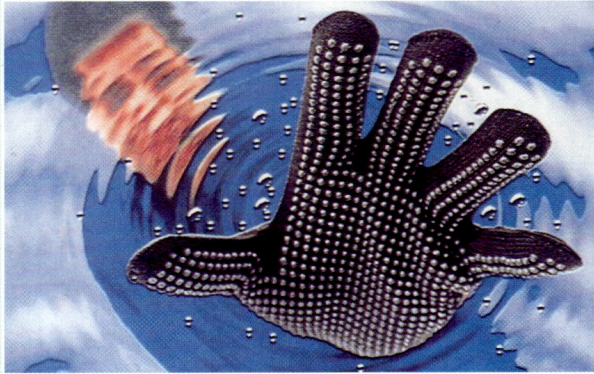

These SealSkinz waterproof MVT gloves are made from a three-layer textile, using CoolMax inside, a breathable membrane in the middle and an outer layer of nylon/polyester/Lycra knit. The gloves will keep your hands warm and dry. You can even string a fishing line or tie a climbing rope without taking them off!

Choosing appropriate textile materials

You will be expected to research the properties of different fibres and fabrics when choosing materials. Be specific in your manufacturing proposal about the best available fabrics and components for the task.

◆ What are the functional and aesthetic properties of the materials you need to make your design?
◆ What properties are essential and which are useful?
◆ What textiles, threads or components are suitable for the task?
◆ Are your chosen materials easy to use?
◆ How much will they cost?
◆ What are the cost implications of using better quality materials?
◆ Can you use any standard components?

Case study: Tri-Aura

'Tri-Aura' is an interactive work designed by artist Frances Geesin and sound engineer Ron Geesin. Computer engineer Spencer Child helped to create this innovative 'hands-on' sound sculpture based on the theme of Earth, Fire and Water. The work is textile-based and uses 'Ultra' fabric made from wool, acrylic and PVC which was originally manufactured for firemen's harnesses. Tri-Aura is contoured and electroplated in copper and nickel. The metallised areas sense and respond to body presence and movement, converting it into light and sound – Tri-Aura sings and glows!

Tri-Aura was commissioned by the Science Museum to celebrate the opening of the major new Challenge of Materials gallery. Tri-Aura is the first protoype exhibit to be put on public display and tested.

shoulder pads

cotton or synthetic webbing for stiffening

belt clip

threads

buttons

zip for convenience

trouser kick tape for strength

nylon hanger loops

stay tapes for reinforcement

fusible 'non-roll' waistband interlining for strength

elastic for easy fit

belt loop tape for stiffening

pocketings

nylon seam binding for pocket strength

fly lining

fusible web adhesive for fusing turn-ups

A variety of components is used in the construction of a man's suit to enhance its style and performance.

Case study: DuPont's new Tactel/Gore-tex fabric

Many sports clothes are made from one type of textile, such as polyester fleece, suitable for several different sports. Nowadays textiles are being engineered to match the performance requirements of individual sports.

The manufacturers DuPont, Gore-tex and Sprayway have jointly developed a new high-performance mountain-wear fabric. The target specifications were designed to meet the market needs for a lighter-weight high-performance fabric. 'Climbers don't want to drag extra weight up a mountain, but they need a high-performance, strong, abrasion-resistant and comfortable fabric,' says Malcolm Woods of DuPont Nylon's Textiles Centre.

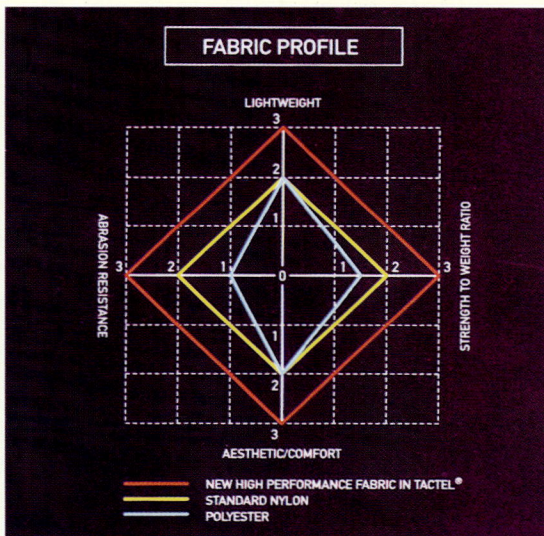

FABRIC PROFILE

LIGHTWEIGHT

ABRASION RESISTANCE

STRENGTH TO WEIGHT RATIO

AESTHETIC/COMFORT

NEW HIGH PERFORMANCE FABRIC IN TACTEL®
STANDARD NYLON
POLYESTER

This diagram shows the properties of the new high-performance Tactel/Gore-tex fabric compared with standard nylon or polyester fabrics.

Focused task: Formulating a fabric specification

In many sports, people may not be wearing the right kind of garments to meet functional and aesthetic requirements. If you are choosing a sports fabric, you could look at what happens to the body in different sports to see if the garments already available are suitable.

- What textile properties are needed?
- Could existing garments be improved?
- Draw up a fabric profile to compare the fabrics available to you.

Exploring textile techniques

Materials can be used in the form in which they are supplied. Alternatively, experimenting with various techniques can inspire more inventive ways of using them.

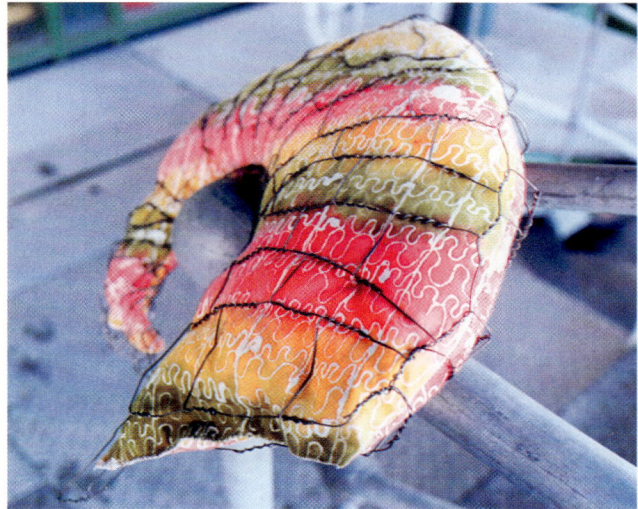

This textile structure by Kulveer was based on a shell. It is made from a batik cushion and binding wire.

Combining, layering, distressing or embellishing textile materials can improve the appearance, handle or performance of a product. You could use simple or complex layering techniques to enhance your textile. For example:

- use iron-on interfacing to strengthen
- use a wadding layer for quilting and insulation
- combine fabric layers for a reversible material
- laminate fabrics with foam or plastic to enhance properties
- spray on a coating for stain, wind or water resistance.

Exploring textile techniques

Stretch your imagination with packaging materials like bubblewrap, made from polythene in two sizes of bubble, 10 ml and 20 ml. This student designed and constructed a jacket. Here are his practical tips when working with bubblewrap.

- Allow room for movement, because bubblewrap is not strong like conventional textiles.
- Pop the bubbles along the seam line before stitching.
- Bind seams with tape or bias binding to give them strength.
- Bound seams can be a design feature (this jacket was made to be reversible).
- Velcro can make a successful fastening.
- Add colour by embroidery or dye.
- Apply glue to the surface and sprinkle with glitter in stripes, checks, a motif or just on the sleeves.
- Pop the bubbles to create a surface pattern of raised and flat areas.

Try making textile products from unusual materials.

Distressing techniques

You can distress fabric and paper to change their appearance, colour and texture. The more you experiment, the more exciting effects you can create.

- Distress fabric by brushing with a stiff wire brush to break down the surface and fray the edges.
- Create lovely effects by layering together dyed muslin, stitching and cutting through the layers, then brushing the surface.
- Brown parcel paper can be brushed with wallpaper paste and scrunched up to soften it. Rub paint, inks or polish into the wet paper and glue tissue paper shapes on to it. When the paper is dry you can rub more colour into it, then stitch it.

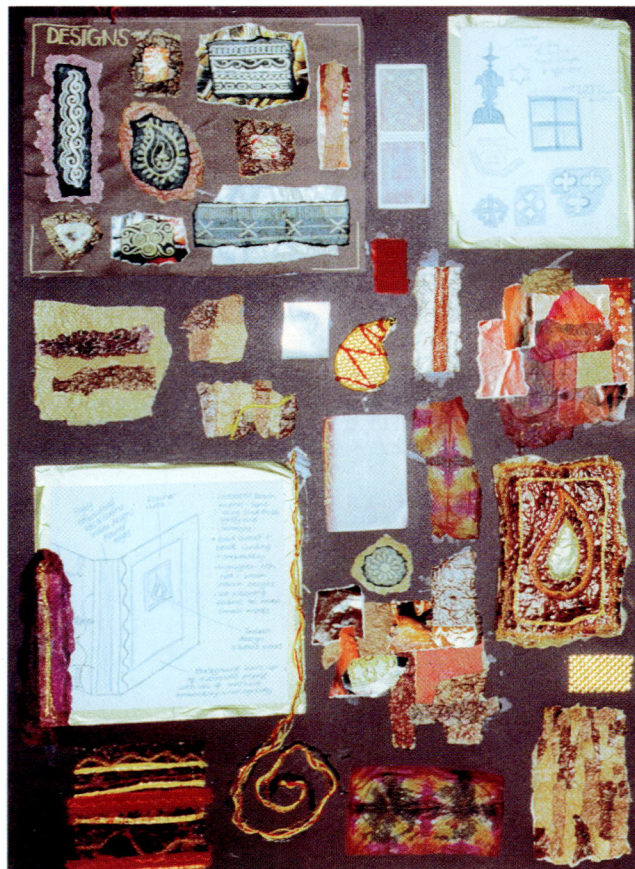

Experimental work with distressing techniques.

Dyed and sculpted textiles

Charlie's bowl was made with dyed muslin that was tied round a tube. The petals were cut out and the edges stitched with threads and wire.

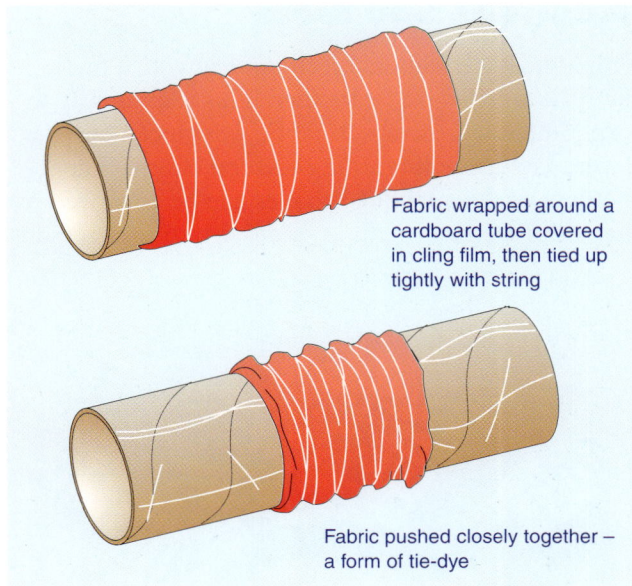

Fabric wrapped around a cardboard tube covered in cling film, then tied up tightly with string

Fabric pushed closely together – a form of tie-dye

You can dye muslin fabric and **sculpt** it at the same time to create 3D textile products.

◆ Wrap fabric round a tube covered in cling-film. Tie it tightly with string and scrunch it up together.
◆ Paint dye and diluted PVA glue on to the fabric. Mix the colours as you paint on the dye to create a rainbow effect.
◆ Allow the fabric to dry. Cut the string and take the fabric off the cardboard tube. It will retain its crinkled effect and be stiff enough to hold its shape.
◆ Stitch wire into the fabric to make it even stiffer.

Machine embroidery

Use machine embroidery to add texture with stitches, threads and fabrics. Create stiff and rigid fabrics with close stitches, or use light open-work.

◆ Different coloured threads will create a speckled effect with subtle colour changes. Matching threads give intense colour.
◆ Experiment with altering the top tension on the machine. Best effects may be found on the back of the fabric.
◆ Use an embroidery hoop, an embroidery or darning foot and drop the feed dogs. Stitch in any direction, using the machine as a drawing tool.
◆ Incorporate yarn, fabrics or cords by zigzag stitching over them. Vary the stitch length to show or hide attached materials.
◆ Stitch small pieces of textured fabric and paper into your work.

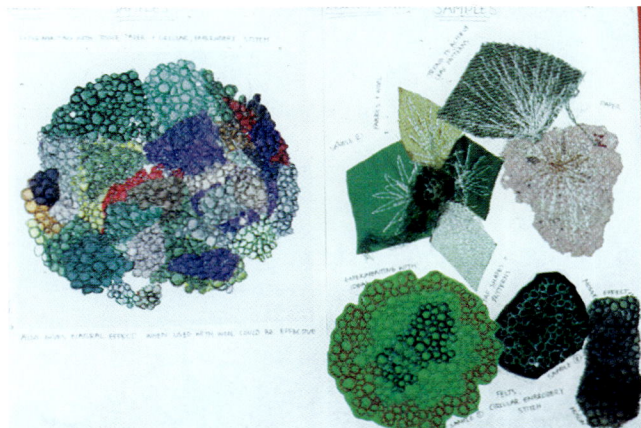

Jo experimented with machine embroidery on different materials, including paper and hand-made felt.

Exploring textile techniques

Appliqué and mola

Appliqué is a traditional technique in which one fabric is stitched on to another. This is a fun way to experiment with scraps of fabric, which can be layered to create interesting textural effects. The outlines of the appliquéd shapes can be enhanced by hand or machine stitching, beads, buttons or sequins.

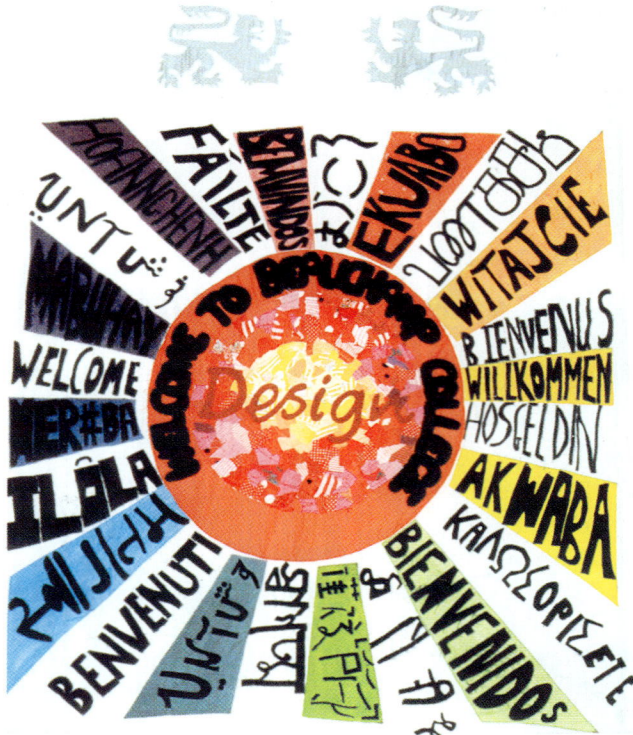

This college banner in 24 languages was a joint project by Year 10 students.

Mola is a form of reverse appliqué. Plan your design on paper using three or more colours then:

- ◆ pin together three or more fabric layers, matching the colours in your design
- ◆ pin and tack a tracing of the design outline on the wrong side of the fabrics
- ◆ machine around the outlines and turn the work to the right side
- ◆ cut layers of fabric away to show the other coloured fabric layers below.

Hand-made felt

Emily's hand-made felt embellished with machine embroidery.

Felt can be made by shrinking and matting fleece in very hot water to form a solid, dense fabric. Use black, dark-brown or white fleece dyed with specialist dyes. Felt can be used as a background for embroidery, or to experiment with other embellishment techniques.

- ◆ Soak fleece in warm water and washing-up liquid to remove grease and dirt. Rinse in clean water, dry and comb the fleece fibres in one direction, then lay on newspaper.
- ◆ Add a design to the base felt with coloured fleece or yarn.
- ◆ Cover the felt with a large piece of cotton fabric and newspaper. Turn it over and add combed fleece to the back, at right angles to the first layer.
- ◆ Drizzle the fleece with washing-up liquid and hot water, then roll it round a broom handle, adding more hot water.
- ◆ Tie the fleece with strong yarn and roll on a flat surface for ten minutes, adding very hot water (wear rubber gloves!). Squeeze out the cooled water and roll for another five to ten minutes, adding more hot water. Do not over roll the felt, which makes it hard and uneven. Press the felt with a hot iron to dry and flatten it.

Design research

Good research will help you to design and make innovative textiles products that people really need. Research can be a very costly activity, so manufacturers have to ensure that it is relevant and used effectively. You need to make sure that your research will help you make the right decisions about designing and making your textile product.

Textile product manufacturers use research to find out the needs and preferences of their customers, as well as other criteria such as:

◆ product function, safety, colour and style
◆ customers' age and size range
◆ properties, safety and availability of fabrics and trimmings
◆ cost and ease of manufacture.

▶ D&T Routes Core Book, Using your research, page 90

Case study: *Using research at Cheryl Playclothes*

Cheryl Playclothes design and manufacture a range of children's play clothes and accessories. Designer Angela Gaskell was asked to create new designs for an 'American Indian' costume which needed to be more traditional and appeal to children. Angela put together a storyboard based on careful research.

fire-retardant fabric

specially designed decorative braid

elasticated trouser waistband for better fit

traditional Indian colours

laced-up tunic provides adaptable sizing

curved front edges of the tunic were changed to straight edges with fringing to simplify production

trousers with an apron front

Images of traditional patterns and photographs of today's native Americans were used to create an 'Indian Inspirations' storyboard.

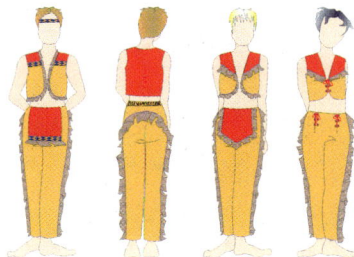

The designer used computer software to develop her ideas. She combined features from her range of designs to create the final playsuit idea.

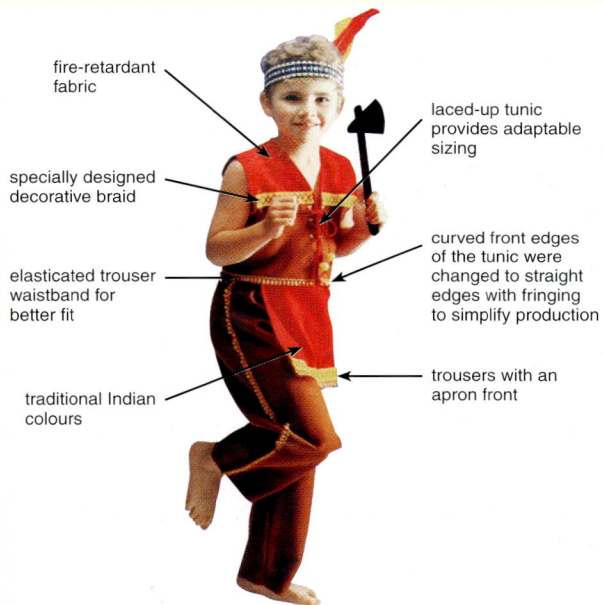

The storyboard gave her ideas for patterns and shapes for a decorative braid which would help to create a more authentic cultural style. The colours had to be attractive to children, so Angela chose reds and yellows based on traditional American Indian colours. Angela also found out that she had to give a high priority to safety when designing the costume. The fabric had to be fire-retardant, wear well, hang well and be easy to care for, as well as appealing to children.

The style of a skirt bottom was thought to reflect native American tradition, but the idea was discarded because many boys in a Western culture might be reluctant to wear one. Instead a compromise was reached, and the trousers have an apron front to make the playsuit more authentic and give it wider appeal. The designs needed to be simplified to reduce the costs of production. Special guides were made for machines to fold the fabric during the making process to ensure quality control and uniformity.

DESIGNING

Modelling and prototyping

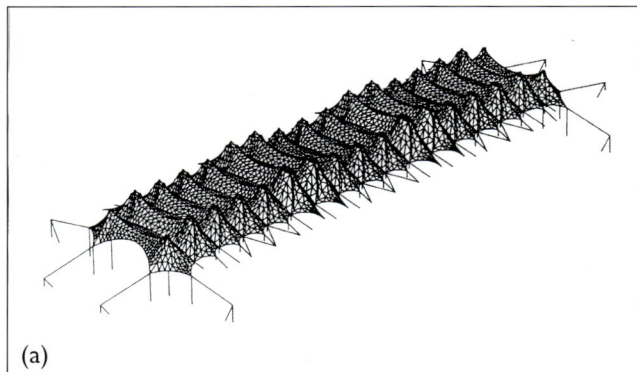
(a)

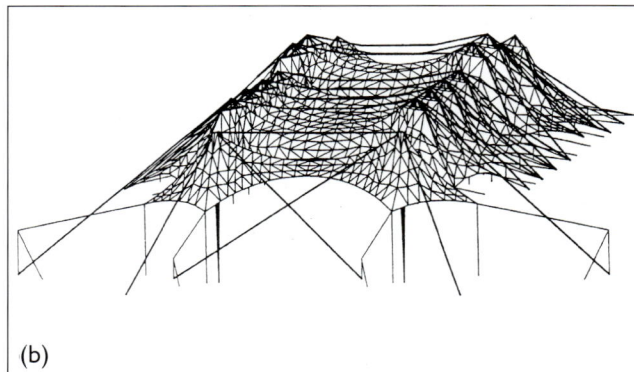
(b)

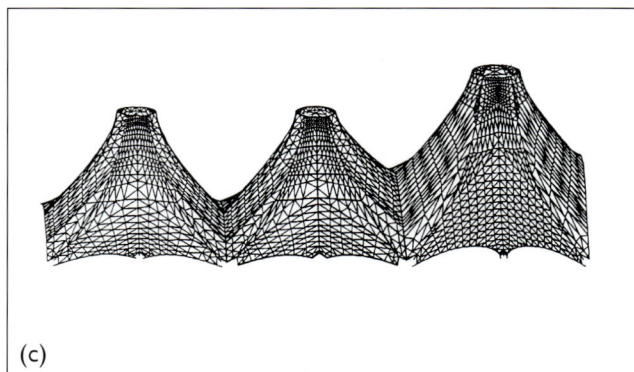
(c)

CAD pictures used to model the new Denver International Airport, which has a fabric roof measuring 300 m × 100 m supported by 34 masts.
a) A coarse mesh model used to work out the overall structure.
b) An installation model used to design the temporary rigging used during construction.
c) A fine mesh pattern model used to generate the shapes for cutting the fabric.

Modelling means visualising your design ideas using hand or computer techniques in two or three dimensions (2D and 3D). A great deal of effort is put in to modelling ideas by designers, as it is a key part of the design process. When modelling textile designs you can:

◆ trial design ideas
◆ experiment with colourways
◆ simulate fabrics and products
◆ present designs and moodboards for evaluation
◆ try out construction methods
◆ test a pattern by making a 'toile' or prototype
◆ see how materials behave
◆ work out a lay plan and costing.

Computer-generated fabrics can be mapped on to garment designs that have been scanned into the computer. The drape of the fabric can be simulated by building a grid around the garment, on to which the fabric or colour is draped.

▶ **D&T Routes Core Book**
Modelling, page 96

58

You should be able to use drawings or CAD to model ideas in 2D. Computer software can be used to create sketches and illustrations and to change colours and patterns, though many designers still prefer to draw by hand. You can use 2D modelling to produce fabric and product ideas which can be presented on a moodboard. This could enable clients to visualise your ideas and choose which they would like to be worked up into a full sample.

(1) Theoretical 3D form   (2) 2D pattern   (3) 3D knitted fabric

Manual pattern construction

Flat patterns are used to construct 3D shapes.

3D modelling is a useful tool which can be used to test a pattern, try out the order of construction and evaluate the suitability of a chosen fabric. A garment designer can develop a pattern by adapting a standard body 'block' or shape. You can use and adapt a commercial pattern, or draw out your own pattern based on the measurements in your working drawing.

You can make a prototype in newspaper to try out your pattern, then make a sample product or toile in inexpensive fabric that matches the properties of your chosen material. This will help you evaluate the success of your design and the suitability of your chosen fabric. It gives you the chance to identify any problems and adapt the pattern if necessary.

Modelling your product thoroughly also means you can work out the order of construction and match it to your method of production.

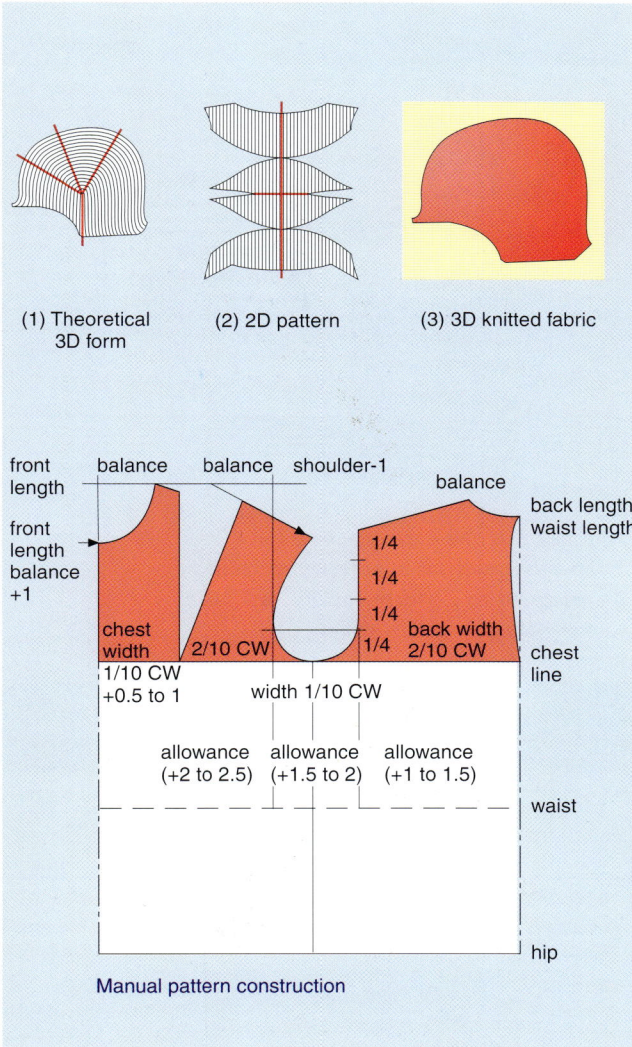

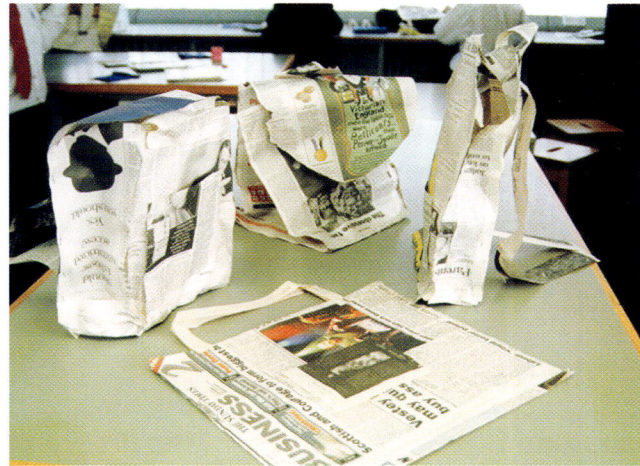

Prototype bags made from newspaper.

Focused task: Creating a design

- Create a design for a textile product such as a waistcoat or bag. Model your design in newspaper using pins or masking tape to hold it together.
- Evaluate your design and identify any problems, making adaptations to your model.
- Use your successful model as a pattern. Carefully undo the pieces and lay the pattern on to your prototype fabric. Don't forget to add seam allowance. Work out the most efficient lay plan so you waste as little fabric as possible.
- Work out the materials needed and costs – you could use a spreadsheet for this.
- Make a flow chart to show the order of making, including critical control points and feedback loops.
- Make up your prototype.

You could visit a factory to see how industrial production differs from yours.

Designing for manufacture

Textile designers do a range of jobs, such as creating yarns, fabrics, garments, household goods or technical textiles. Each type of job needs specialist equipment and different manufacturing processes, so the designer needs to have a good working knowledge of them. A successful designer is a creative artist and a skilled technician.

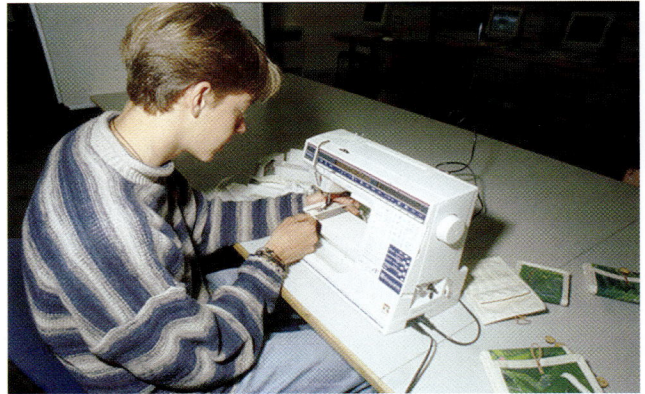

> D&T Routes Core Book,
> **Designing for manufacture**
> **pages 103–105**

There are over 6000 types of sewing-machine needle, so choosing one suitable for the job is most important. These needles are unique because the eye and thread-carrying groove are die-pressed, to combat breakage and slip-stitching.

As a student designer you could work with a range of equipment, such as a computer-aided plotter-cutter, an overlocker, or screen-printing equipment. You need to produce a quality textile product that can be easily made, so you need to think about:

◆ the availability and suitability of the equipment
◆ the limitations set by the equipment
◆ the skills needed to use the equipment.

The processes you use can affect your product design and cost, so think about the kind of production you will use. It could be one-off or high-volume production.

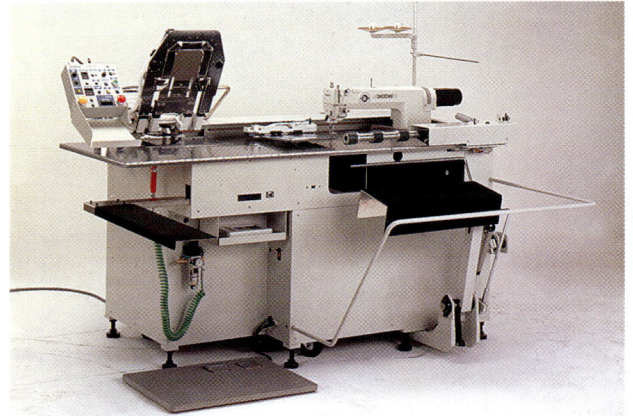

You may use one basic machine for a number of tasks but in industry machines are designed to perform specific tasks like button-holing or collar-making.

Focused task: Designing for manufacture

You have been asked to design a range of accessories, such as belts, hats or scarves. Sketch your ideas for a specific client group. Your designs must be quick and easy to manufacture in high volume. Record what changes you make to your design and why. Make a flow chart of the manufacturing processes required and equipment needed.

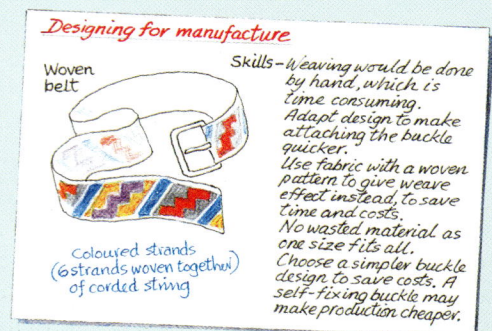

Designing for manufacture

Woven belt

Coloured strands (6 strands woven together) of corded string

Skills – Weaving would be done by hand, which is time consuming. Adapt design to make attaching the buckle quicker.
Use fabric with a woven pattern to give weave effect instead, to save time and costs.
No wasted material as one size fits all.
Choose a simpler buckle design to save costs. A self-fixing buckle may make production cheaper.

Taking ideas into production, page 62

Communicating designs

When you present your ideas to a client your aim is to attract their interest and sell them your idea. A design presented in an imaginative way is more likely to be eye-catching and appealing. You can make your design more exciting by using an unusual composition, and by the use of different media or techniques.

Students from Ordsall Hall School presented their ideas to clients in the company.

Techniques for presentation

Media such as paint, coloured inks, chalk and oil pastels, coloured pencils, paper collage and felt-tips can be used to present your ideas. Here are some techniques you can try.

◆ A photocopied or scanned image can be transferred on to acetate and laid over a textured background or another image. This is an interesting way to add notes to your image.

◆ Fabric samples can be cut with pinking shears or can have the edges fringed. Samples can be placed behind window mounts that are shaped to reflect patterns in the design.

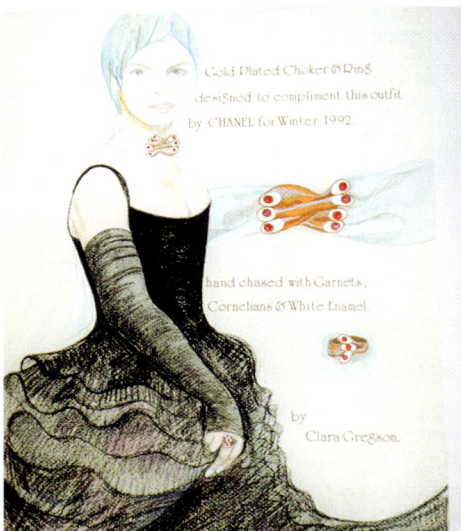

You could show your design in the situation in which it is going to be used.

Focused task: Presentation

Fashion designers often promote their work through advertisements in glossy magazines. You could present your design in the format of a magazine advertisement. You could:

■ create an image of your design using your chosen media
■ photograph the image and scan into a computer
■ experiment with scale, proportion and colours using computer software (such as Micrografix Designer)
■ add text to your design image.

Case study: Video cataloguing

New technology is providing the opportunity for interior textile manufacturers, design shops and interiors architects to present textiles like curtains or upholstery to potential customers. For example, shops can use video cataloguing as a point-of-sale system to enable a customer to search for a design and colourways from a library of fabric designs. These collections can be shown in realistic room settings, with fabric designs mapped on to furniture, flooring, curtains, and even wallpaper.

Stop and think

In future you may not have to visit a shop to see textile products – you could view them at home using a PC. What impact would this have on people's lifestyles and employment possibilities?

Add a touch of fantasy by showing your design in an unusual situation. Harjinda thought her finished woven sculpture looked crab-like, so she presented it on a seashore. She made a collage using paper, coloured inks, yarn and sand.

MANUFACTURING

Taking ideas into production

A product is manufactured in large quantities so that it can be widely available at a low unit cost. When designing for high-volume manufacture, economy in production is vital, including consideration of the appearance of the product, its end function, the use of the least possible resources, and so on. This will determine the final cost and saleability of the product, and is only achieved through thorough investigation during the design development and production planning stages. Any manufacturing problems should be sorted out, choosing the most efficient production route which gives the best and most cost-effective results.

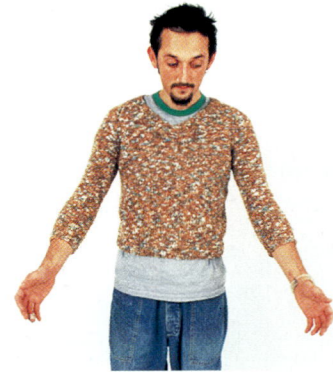

The sweater that didn't meet its design specification!

> ### Stop and think
>
> The designer of the sweater obviously got something wrong.
>
> What went wrong?
> - Why do you think this happened?
> - At what stage do you think it could have been prevented?

▶ **Design specification page 21**

As more women take up sport, the medical world has stressed a need for better bust support. Berlei has reacted by specifying a range of bras for different levels of sporting activity.

At the beginning of a project, a **design specification** detailing the requirements of the product will usually be discussed and drawn up between the designer and the client. This specification can change during design development, but not so drastically for the product to not meet the client's requirements or its purpose. Throughout the development stage several prototypes may be made, giving an idea of how the design will look and how it will be manufactured.

▶ **Testing, page 66**

Sourcing

The materials and components for your design must be planned in advance as finding suitable ones can be difficult, especially if the product is to be made in large quantities. It is no good finding the ideal zip-fastener for a bag if it is not available in the quantities you need to fulfil your orders. Likewise, using a cheaper fabric will only save you money if it meets all the design specifications. Saving money by using cheaper components may cost more money in the long term, if they don't perform as they should.

Quality, cost and design are all essential for the success of a product manufactured in volume. A product that is both well designed and well made may not sell if the selling price is too high, equally a good design can fail if the quality is below customers' expectations.

Things to consider when designing for high volume production.

◆ **Equipment** – what equipment is required and is it available? Will new tools be required? How much will they cost?

- **Skills** – what skills are required? Do you have them? Is the design suitable for easy assembly in production?
- **Processes** – what processes do you need to undertake? How complex are they? How long will they take? Is it possible to reduce the production time? Can you use a machine to speed up production?

- **Materials** – are the materials readily available? Is it possible to reduce the number of parts and different materials used? Can you reduce the amount of waste material? Can you use standard parts?
- **Quality** – Is it possible to make a high volume of products and keep the quality the same on each product? How will this be assured?
- **Cost** – can it be made for an acceptable price?

Case study: Brunts School and Pilgrim Textiles, Mansfield

Pilgrim Textiles is a company manufacturing for a mail-order catalogue. Through research they discovered that there was a market for school-leavers starting work who found it difficult to budget for clothing. They wanted a range aimed at the teenage market which would provide a service enabling young people to pay for their clothes in manageable, regular amounts. Students at Brunts School were asked by the company to design a range of garments to be included in a mail-order catalogue which fulfilled the requirements of young people starting work. As part of this project, the students had to think carefully about the difference between designing garments which were one-off and those which would be manufactured in high volume.

Low volume		High volume	
1. Product by individual craftsperson	Making a garment from a paper pattern, one person doing the whole process	Forming a production line or cell, with a team to produce garments	1. Team based product
2. Project limited by personal finance	Using materials available at school	Buying materials in bulk, each component of garment precisely costed to ensure profit	2. Project controlled by more precise costing
3. Manufacturing quality based on craft skill	Quality is checked as it is made and mistakes corrected as work progresses	Quality is checked at critical points in manufacture. Computer-aided manufacture used	3. Manufacturing quality is more reliant on systems and control
4. Hand tools predominate	Using tools and machinery available at school	Made using programmable machinery	4. Greater reliance on programmable machine tools
5. Quality control is in the hands of the designer/maker	Use your specification to guide quality, evaluate as you progress	Use a manufacturing specification. Compare to finished sample. Check for product safety and suitability for end use	5. Quality is more tightly controlled through specific use of quality systems (QA, QC, TQM, CI)

- Write down what you think the requirements for the Pilgrim products would be and draw up a checklist that could be used as a design specification.
- Make a checklist of the manufacturing considerations if these are going to be made in high volume.

- Describe what the differences between making in low volume and high volume would be. You can use a chart to help you.

D&T Routes Core Book
Methods of production, page 120

Developing a manufacturing specification

To ensure that a product is manufactured exactly as the designer intended, and that each one is made identically to the next, a **manufacturing specification sheet** is drawn up. All the design details and making instructions are written down with a detailed drawing, including the materials used, component parts, measurements, manufacturing processes and finishing details.

The manufacturing specification needs to be very clear and accurate for the design to be reproduced as the designer originally intended. Every manufacturing company's system of recording this information will differ in layout but will include similar information.

This checklist includes all the information you should have in a specification.

◆ Front, back and side views of the product.
◆ Clear design details, with magnified drawing of some if necessary.
◆ Clear construction details, showing what type of stitches and where they will go. You may need to illustrate this.
◆ Dimensions of the product – including finished length, width, height, and so on.
◆ Details of materials – you will need to include sample of material and colourway. You will sometimes need to include the name of the supplier.
◆ Details of components - for example, size and quantity of buttons or studs, length and type of zip, length and width of elastic, and so on.

MANUFACTURING SPECIFICATION
DESCRIPTION: Expedition Vest with **Buoyancy Aid CE Certification**

Sizes: Ladies/Youth; Gents
Dimension Data for Flotation Foam:

	a	b	c	d
Ladies/Youth	36cm	31cm	19cm	41cm
Gents	39cm	33cm	19cm	42cm

Size & Flotation Data:

	Ladies / Youth	Gents
Height	140-175cm	170-190cm
Chest Size	80-108cm	92-122cm
Body Weight	45-65kg	60-85kg
Flotation	>65N	>70N

Shell Fabric:
Outer: Murmar Fabrics 500 Denier Cordura. CE Approved.
Inner: William Reeds 4 oz. Nylon. CE Approved.

Flotation Foam:
Zote Foams LD24 Expanded Polyethylene. Multiple layers of 10mm thickness or Vitacell 7/50 soft PVC foam. CE Approved.

Sewing Thread: 60's bonded nylon. **Seam Allowances:** 10mm

Elastics: **Side:** Jones & Co. E20 25mm elastic

Safety Harness & Cowstall:
Harness: 50mm Rykneld Tean Polypropylene Webbing. 50mm Fixlock Cam Buckle with Seasure Products Stainless Steel plate.
Cowstall: Mammut Sport Tubular 25mm Webbing with Jones & Co. E5 16mm Elastic Inner. DMM CE Approved Truklip 70kN Karabiner. Seasure Products Stainless Steel D-ring.

Webbing:
Shoulder: Rykneld Tean Ltd. 25mm Polypropylene adjusters. 40mm Polypropylene Shoulder
Side: Rykneld Tean Ltd. 25mm Polyproylene. **Waist:** Rykneld Tean Ltd. 20mm Polypropylene

Buckles:
Shoulder: homa Locks 25mm Ladder Locks. **Side:** Homa Locks 25mm Ladder Locks.
Waist: Homa Locks 20mm Ladder Locks. Also webbing plate for attaching knife or pocket.

Logo & Labelling: BSB Two Colour Large Peak Transfer. Embroidered Peak Label. Care & Fitting Instruction Label and swing ticket.

These examples each show a garment manufacturer's specification sheet which a designer has written. The information will be used by the pattern technician to cut the pattern, and the sample technician who will produce the first sample. If the sample passes the quality checks, this specification can then be used as the quality standards in the mass production of the product.

DESIGN DETAIL SHEET/MANUFACTURING SPECIFICATION
DATE: 23.3.97
DESIGN NO.: 5.403
DESIGNER: D.F.
CUSTOMER: TOP BOD.
SIZE: MEDIUM

WRITTEN DESCRIPTION: CROPPED T-SHIRT - STRIPE 2 x 2cm VERTICAL RIB NECK - WHITE - 1 x 1

FRONT & BACK VIEW

* O/L SHOULDER SEAMS
* O/L CUFFS TO SLEEVES
* O/L SLEEVES INTO ARMHOLES
* O/L SIDE SEAM & UNDERARMS
* O/L NECK IN.
* COVERSEAM HEM.

DESCRIPTION	SIZE	DESCRIPTION	SUPPLIER	NO.	WIDTH	COST	GARMENT PIECE
A LENGTH	33cm	100% COTTON	OLYMPIAN	x3019	165	£8.95	ALL
B CHEST	44	SINGLE JERSEY					
C HEM CIRC.	44						
D ARMHOLE	19						
E UNDERARM	15						
F CUFF	14						
G NECK OPENING	15	TRIMS					
H BACK NECK DEPTH	3	1 x 1 RIB	OLYMPIAN	R4310	45	3.75	NECK/CUFFS
I FRONT " "	6.5						
J SHOULDER	15						
K NECK RIB DEPTH	2						

GARMENT DETAILS / FABRIC DETAILS

D&T Routes Core Book
Manufacturing specification, page 147

Take a simple textile product, such as a soft toy, fabric bag or jacket. Use the checklist to make a manufacturing specification for the product. This should show exactly how to make it and what materials are needed. If you followed the specification and made the item it would be exactly like the product you have chosen.

DESIGN DETAIL SHEET. TIPS PROJECT - ASHFIELD SCHOOL/MARTINS

An example of a student's specification sheet showing details of a V-neck shirt design.

Using computer software to produce manufacturing specifications

Specification sheets are often produced on computer. New CAD technology is making it easier and quicker for the designer to produce accurate manufacturing specifications. Could you use a computer to help you with your specification?

Focused task: *Manufacturing specification for sportswear*

Using the examples shown, produce a manufacturing specification sheet for a design for a new type of sports shorts or shirt. The information you record can be used to plan the production of your item, and to help standardise the quality of each one made.

- Could someone else produce your design from the information you have provided?
- Have you included all the dimensions required?
- Are details of all materials and accessories shown?
- Have you given clear making-up instructions.
- Is it clear how the product should look when finished?

Using Style Manager software.

Testing before production

A number of prototype products will be made before the final sample is manufactured in large quantities. This ensures that the final product meets the requirements of the customer, is fit for its intended purpose, and will perform in the conditions for which it is designed.

Each prototype is tested to ensure all the performance criteria are met. These may include durability, aftercare conditions and the product's performance in certain conditions, and may be simple or very complex using high-tech computer-controlled equipment. Whatever type of tests are used, it is important to ensure that exactly the same conditions and procedures are maintained every time the test is carried out. If the product has to conform to certain established British or European Standards, such as in the case of furnishings, children's clothing and nightwear, each test must comply with the guidelines provided by the standards authority.

Testing components and materials

Testing for abrasion resistance.

The continual contact of a fabric's surface with another surface can cause 'bobbling' or 'pilling' to occur. This machine simulates the contact a sock would have with a shoe over a period of time. As some fibres pill less than others, the appearance of the fabric or garment can be tested and compared.

Some products require a fabric to perform well under harsh conditions, particularly those that are used in garments to protect the body, such as wetsuits. The machine shown above right is testing the tear strength of such a fabric.

Colour is particularly important in fashion items. Every component, including fabric, buttons and

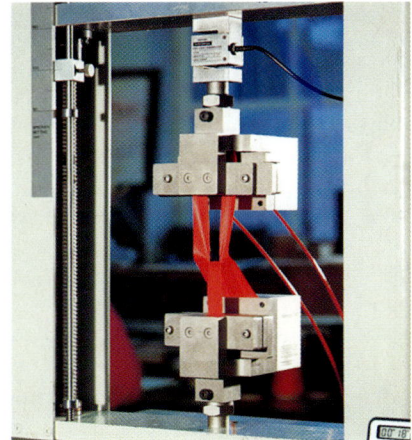

Testing tear strength.

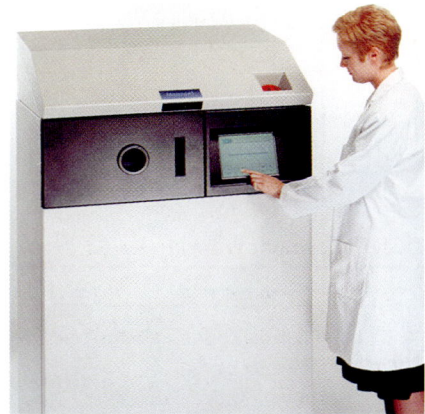

Testing colour fastness.

threads, must be tested against a standard to ensure it is exactly the right colour under different lighting conditions, such as daylight, tungsten lighting and shop lighting. Each component must be 'colourfast' and not lose colour when washed unless this is an intended feature (for example, a pair of jeans is designed to fade when washed). If the product is to be exposed to continual daylight and weather conditions, such as a tent, fabric is tested under accelerated weather and fading conditions using complex computer-controlled equipment.

Components are tested to determine their suitability. A wide number of tests can be carried out, depending upon the end requirements.

Testing the product

Once the materials and components of the product have been identified, an initial prototype is made and tested. The manufacturer may wish to try out new or improved methods of manufacturing, and in this case a production trial may be undertaken.

The prototype is tested under the conditions in which it will be used. The aim of this is to evaluate how it meets the demands of the customer and environment in terms of performance, durability, appearance and cost. All characteristics of the product will be tested, including the joining processes, to determine their suitability.

Once in production, routine tests will be undertaken to ensure quality standards are maintained.

▶ Quality, page 81

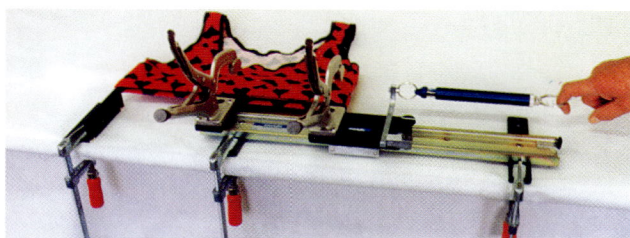

Here the strength and elasticity of a seam in a stretch garment is being tested.

Focused task: Performance testing

Carpets and upholstery are tested to give a performance rating against a British Standard. For example, carpets can be certified as suitable for:

- heavy non-domestic use
- heavy domestic use
- general domestic use
- moderate domestic use.

1 Explain what you think each category means.

2 If you were designing a carpet for the following situations, for which category would it need to pass the test?

- A stair carpet for an office complex.
- A bedroom carpet.
- A carpet for a school.

3 Below is a list of tests.

tensile and tear strength	'Hexapod Walker' test
burst strength	foam ageing
flammability	abrasion resistance
seam slippage	colour and light fastness
stretch and recovery	oiling resistance
anti-static	

Sort the list out into three groups of tests you might use for:

- carpets ■ upholstery ■ both.

Focused task: Flammability

Domestic fires kill 600 people a year. It is vital that everyday goods are fire-resistant. Flammability tests are carried out by experts who have technical expertise and specialised equipment. Manufacturers are concerned to make sure that they are improving the safety of their products when they design new ones. Here is a list of items which should be tested for flammability by experts to meet British Standards. State why you think each item is on the list.

- Clothing.
- Toys and nursery products.
- Furnishings and upholstery.
- Carpets and curtains.
- Camping and leisure products.
- Seating and soft furnishings of cars, buses, trains, ships and aircraft.

Case study: Samsonite suitcase tests

Samsonite manufactures high-quality luggage that is well known for its strength and durability. Ever since it started in 1910, the company has rigorously tested all its products. Tumble tests, wheel tests, handle tests and drop tests are carried out in Samsonite's own laboratories, to simulate real travel conditions and see how each product will withstand the rough handling it may encounter.

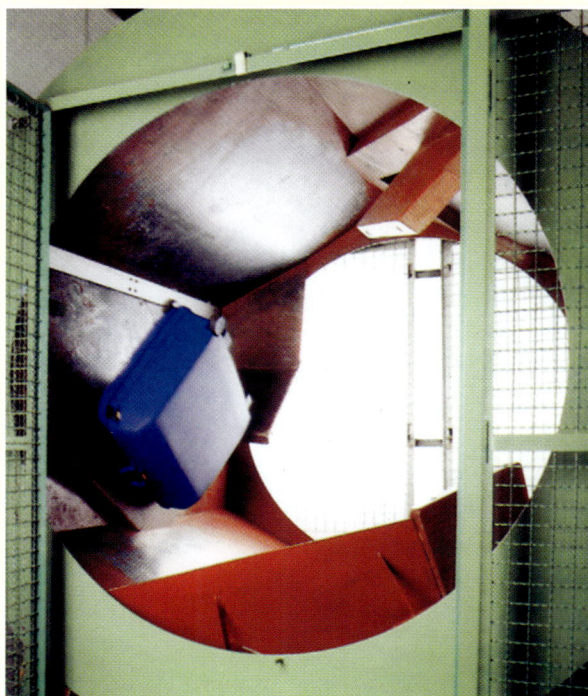

Tumble test

MANUFACTURING

Case study: *Simulated testing in action*

At Leeds University they test the performance of industrial, sports and leisure clothing and helmets, ropes, harnesses and boots. They simulate the conditions and record the results. They have helped test fleeces for Ranulph Fiennes to use on his Antarctic expedition, and to redesign clothes for the police and bags for postal delivery workers.

There is a cold room to test the way temperatures change through a piece of clothing. The garment should be warmer on the inside than the outside, unless the clothing is for very hot climates when it should lose heat. The cold room takes things down to minus 30°C, the extreme temperatures found in the Himalayas and in polar regions. Changes in humidity and temperature are logged using sensors.

There is a rain room which simulates constant drizzle, and subjects garments and equipment to between eight and 30 mm of rain an hour.

Stop and think

- Why are these tests simulated?
- Could you simulate situations to test your design?

Focused task: Designing key tests

When testing a product before manufacturing it is useful to design a series of tests that are linked to the key requirements of the product, and to compare how different components and manufacturing techniques perform under these conditions.

- What would be the key fabric and garment tests required for a skiing jacket?
- How would you go about them in industry, and in the classroom?

Production planning

The Manufacturing Process

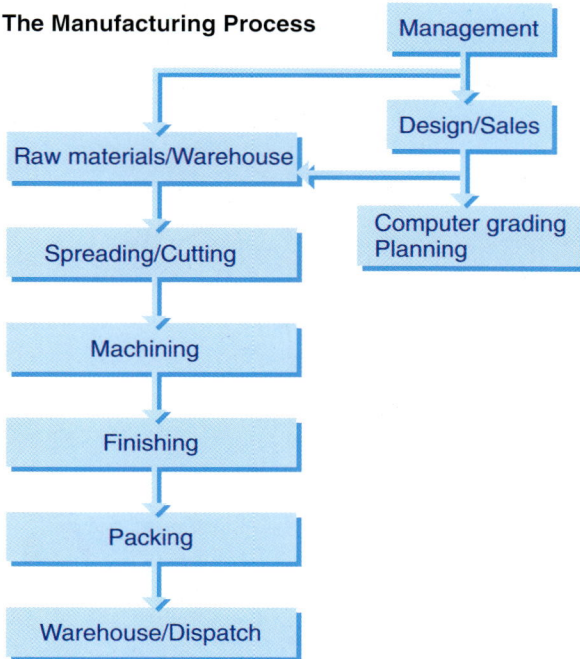

Management → Design/Sales → Computer grading Planning

Management → Raw materials/Warehouse → Spreading/Cutting → Machining → Finishing → Packing → Warehouse/Dispatch

| TIPS PROJECT – CRITICAL PATH |||
| ASHFIELD SCHOOL – PARTNER COMPANY – MARTINS |||
TASK	VENUE	COMPLETION DATE
Factory visit	Martins	Fri 6th Sept 10.45–12.45
Delivery of design brief and guidance on range	School	Fri 13th Sept Period 3
Mood board session (NADCAT)	School	To be arranged possibly Fri 20th Sept 10.30–12.30
Team review (1st presentation)	Martins	Fri 11th Oct 11.45–12.45
Cost analysis	School	Fri 18th Oct Period 3
1st sampling & fit grading of patterns	School	Fri 18th Oct 10.30–12.30 Fri 1st Nov 10.30–12.30
Completion of patterns/toiles	School	Fri 8th Nov Period 3 Fri 15th Nov Period 3 Fri 22nd Nov Period 3 (lunch times available)
Making up of final garments	Martin's sample room	Dec 1996 – Jan 1997 1.30–3.30 Fridays (to be arranged)
Fashion show	Mansfield LC	6th Feb all day

Any manufacturing process involves a sequence of stages rather like this one. In the clothing industry people with particular skills and qualifications undertake specific tasks.

Successful manufacture of a product in high volume relies on efficient **planning** and **monitoring** of all the stages in its production. From when the raw materials arrive to the finished product, each stage must be carefully planned to suit the facilities and resources available. This is sometimes referred to as the **critical path** of a product, which begins with the designer working closely with both the customer and the manufacturer on developing and testing new design ideas.

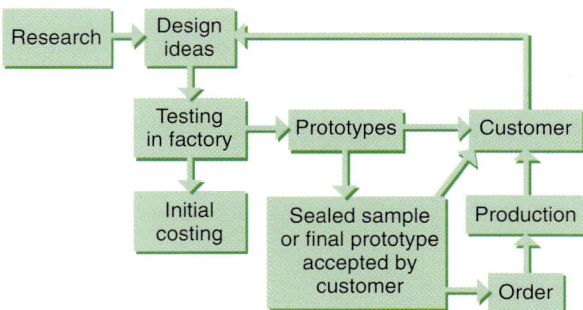

Students planning the production of their own garment design.

Research → Design ideas → Testing in factory → Prototypes → Customer
Design ideas → Customer
Testing in factory → Initial costing → Sealed sample or final prototype accepted by customer → Production → Order → Customer

Above right is the critical path planned for students involved in a garment design and manufacture project. It is similar to that operated by the company the students visited, giving an insight into the route a new product follows in industry.

Focused task: Plan a critical path for your own design

Plan a critical path for your own design. Begin by breaking down the stages and operations in its manufacture and put them in order in the form of a flow chart. You can then see how best to arrange the time you have available to finish the product.

Data management systems

Planning for production of a new product involves collection and analysis of data concerning the product. This is organised through a data management system, which ensures that all necessary materials, services, equipment and information are ready for when the product goes into production.

MANUFACTURING

69

Production planning

Case study: The Sweater Shop

The Sweater Shop is what is known as a vertical company. This means that it carries out the entire process of garment manufacturing – right through from the initial design concept to retailing the finished product. The company therefore needs computerised management systems in all areas to allow efficient running of the business. The system the company uses provides direct links between the design room, the factory and the retail outlets, giving maximum response to customer demands. This system is known as **CIM (computer-integrated manufacture)**, which allows integration of information flow in a company.

CIM systems are used for quick responses to market demands, enabling companies to control and adjust their stock levels according to what is selling in the shops. The systems link the shop tills directly to the manufacturer, giving information on which styles are selling in what quantity, sizes and colourways. The manufacturer can

The Sweater Shop retail outlets use the EPOS computer system, which automatically informs the manufacturer what has been sold.

then release these products from its stock, so the shop does not sell out, or produce more if stocks are running low. Likewise, if a product is not selling well the manufacturer can make a decision on whether or not to continue making it.

JIT – just in time

JIT stands for **just in time**, a phrase used in planning the ordering of materials which are bought in from outside suppliers. Storage of these materials is obviously going to take up valuable space which could be utilised for production. It also ties up money in stock waiting to be used. It is therefore necessary to ensure these materials arrive at the factory just in time for production. Computers have enabled this complex system of organising the ordering and delivery of goods to flow much more efficiently.

Production plan

The production plan will consist of standard forms used to collect the information required for each process, such as:

- design specifications
- manufacturing specifications
- lay plans
- cutting dockets
- work orders
- cost sheets.

Work orders

A work order is the written breakdown of all the operations in the manufacture of a product. It gives instructions on how to assemble the product, in which order, and what equipment is needed. The information is usually condensed, sometimes with abbreviations being used, but for more complicated designs or if the product is the first of a new range it will be explained more fully. These assembly instructions (work orders) are often included in the manufacturing specification.

Focused task: Just in time

Imagine you are in a team which is printing T-shirts for different school occasions. You have been asked to produce T-shirts over the next few months, including:

- a design for the summer school journey
- a design for the Y11 leavers
- a design to raise money for a children's charity.

Write a plan to make sure all necessary materials, services, equipment and information would be ready for when the T-shirts go into production.

- What system could you develop to make sure that your T-shirts use JIT techniques?
- What information could you collect as the T-shirts are sold, and how might you use this to inform your production?

Focused task: Work orders

Produce a work order for your own product, or for the T-shirt from the task on page 24. You can use the system of abbreviations listed below, which are the most common used in the textile industry:

O/L	Overlock	R.S.	Right side
L/S	Lockstitch	W.S.	Wrong side
T/S	Topstitch	Tog.	Together
C/S	Coverseam	L/S R.S. Tog.	Lockstitch right
S/T	Staystitch		sides together.

Different methods of production

When deciding on how you are going to produce your design there are several different methods of manufacture to consider. The type of method is determined by the quantity of articles to be made, and when and how many are to be delivered.

- **Jobbing** or **custom-made**, where only one product is produced. Also known as 'making through'.
- **Batch production**, used for producing larger though fixed quantities of identical products either for stock or to order.
- **Mass production**, where high volumes are produced for stock or to order.
- **Continuous production**, in which very large volumes are produced continuously, and machines run 24 hours a day for weeks, months or years.

Continuous production requires maximum use of machinery and minimum labour, and needs a high level of automation and specialisation. It is unlikely that you will be producing large quantities of your product in school, so your choice will be either jobbing or batch production.

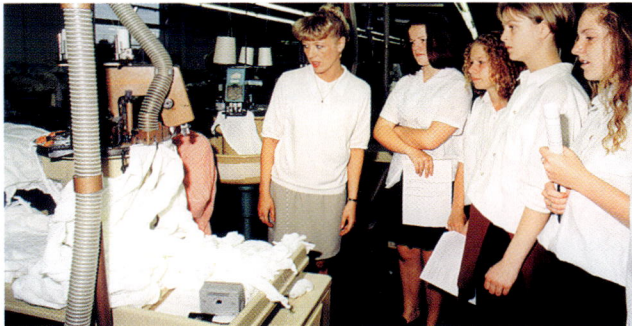

These students were given unwanted fabric by a local knitwear company with which to design and produce a garment or item. They used the same processes as the factory, which meant that the products could be reproduced in a batch if required.

Focused task: Which method of manufacture?

Use the case studies on this page and page 72 to help you decide on a method of manufacture for your product. You will need to think about:

- what quantity is to be produced?
- if only one is to be made, is it a prototype?
- how much time have you got?
- how much will it cost?

One-off production

One-off production is usually carried out on behalf of individual clients, according to their particular requirements. It takes more time to make the item than if it had been mass produced, making it more expensive. But the client ends up with an individual design, unique to them, and made with high-quality materials and workmanship.

Some products are more unusual or the circumstances for which they are designed are unique, such as this roof over Lords Cricket Ground.

Case study: The Logo Carpet Company

The Logo Carpet Company produce one-off carpets for individual customers. The designer uses a CAD/CAM system to transfer the customer's design, often a company logo, into the finished carpet. The first step is scanning the logo into the computer, which then converts the design into warp and weft threads to be reproduced as a carpet.

The customer often orders only one carpet, for their office or for promotional purposes, though occasionally more than one is required in which case this could be called batch production. As the pattern is stored in the CAD/CAM system the design can be reproduced identically every time.

Different methods of production

Northern Diver is Europe's largest manufacturer of made-to-measure neoprene drysuits. The wearer of the suit is completely shielded from the external environment, whatever the tough and often unknown conditions may be. The suits therefore require great skill and expertise in their manufacture.

Each one of the suits is hand-made, and yet it only takes five days to make and deliver to the customer. At any one time up to 200 suits are passing along the production line. This shows well-planned manufacturing. The speed of the made-to-measure service is only made possible with the use of a CAD/CAM system. Each suit is designed, planned and graded on-screen before being transferred to the cutting bed. Adjustments from standard sizes are automatically calculated, and the pattern pieces modified. This automatic size adjusting enables a perfect fit and ensures clean and accurate seam integrity between the pattern pieces. This is imperative for watertight seams, which are constructed using three coats of adhesive.

Northern Diver's design team is constantly testing new materials and designs to enhance the quality and comfort of the suits. This involves continual modification of the patterns, which costs time and money, but it means the company will hopefully remain at the forefront of this market.

You may decide that due to demand you have to produce more than one product, but that each product needs to be slightly different to fit the customer's needs. In this case a standard pattern can be produced that allows for these slight modifications. This will obviously be more costly than producing a batch of identical items, but because of the nature of the product's individual fit you should be able to charge more.

Focused task: One-off production and batch production

Find more examples of products made by one-off production and batch production in the textiles industry:

- explain why each of these products uses this particular method of manufacture.
- when do you use one-off or batch manufacture in your project work?
- what is the difference between making a prototype and making a one-off product?

Producing in volume

Mass production of a product is aimed at a specific target consumer group. Standardised patterns, equipment and manufacturing processes mean that every product is the same and no allowances can be made for individuals. Large-scale manufacturing techniques allow production of a wide range of products in a fraction of the time taken for one-off items, and therefore the products cost less.

Case study: Martin Emprex International

Martin Emprex International produces men's, women's and children's wear for leading high-street retailers. The company uses mass-production systems of manufacture to accommodate the huge range of styles and quantities. The flow of materials through the factory requires effective planning. Smooth flow patterns are important for economic manufacturing.

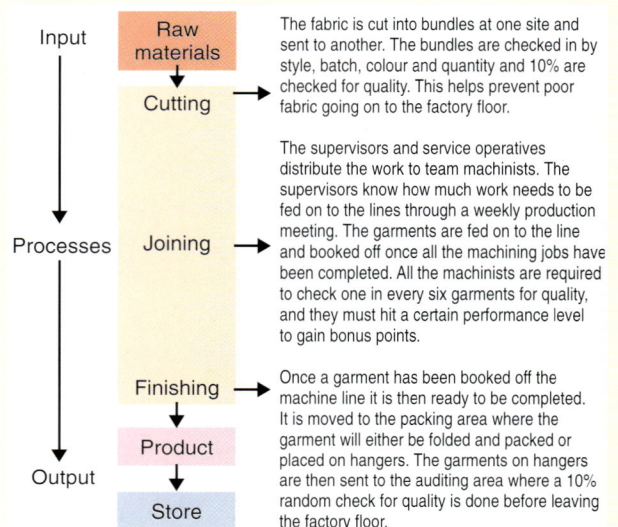

Input — Raw materials — Cutting: The fabric is cut into bundles at one site and sent to another. The bundles are checked in by style, batch, colour and quantity and 10% are checked for quality. This helps prevent poor fabric going on to the factory floor.

Processes — Joining: The supervisors and service operatives distribute the work to team machinists. The supervisors know how much work needs to be fed on to the lines through a weekly production meeting. The garments are fed on to the line and booked off once all the machining jobs have been completed. All the machinists are required to check one in every six garments for quality, and they must hit a certain performance level to gain bonus points.

Finishing — Product: Once a garment has been booked off the machine line it is then ready to be completed. It is moved to the packing area where the garment will either be folded and packed or placed on hangers. The garments on hangers are then sent to the auditing area where a 10% random check for quality is done before leaving the factory floor.

Output — Store

Using CAD/CAM

CAD/CAM has dramatically improved communication between designer, customer and manufacturer. A designer can produce and transmit design ideas, specification sheets and alterations direct to the manufacturer, who can review the design and make any adjustments that may be required for production. This can then be sent back for acceptance by the customer. Final approval can taken hours instead of weeks, making it easier to respond to customer needs and market trends.

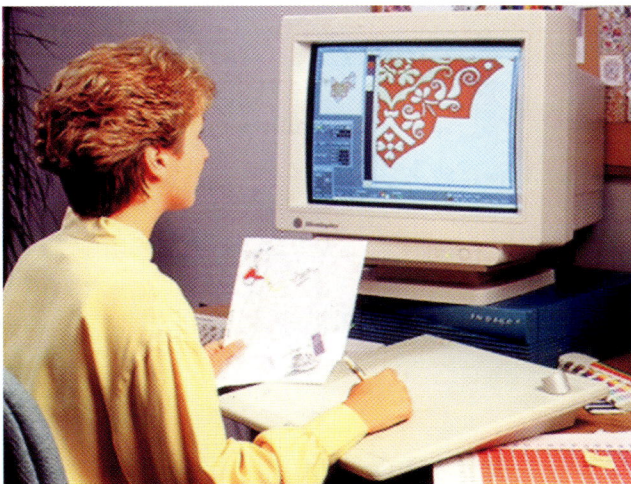

The use of computers in manufacturing

Many of the manufacturing processes within a textile company are now controlled by information technology, from order processing through to despatch, and from automatic cutting and lay planning through to computer-controlled knitting machines.

Gerber manufacture a wide range of computer systems which can control everything within one factory.

These students from Valley School, Worksop, were able to design garments from scratch with the help of a computer programmer from Courtaulds.

73

Different methods of production

Outputting your design ideas

Print a design as a stencil for appliqué, fabric painting or screen-printing.

◆ Design a suitable motif using paint or draw software.
◆ Make a test print to check that the size is correct. Adjust if necessary.
◆ Bear in mind the purpose of the printout. If the shape alone is required (for example, appliqué templates), you can print several motifs on one page and cut them out. If a stencil for spraying is needed then position one motif centrally on the page.
◆ Remember that the paper used to wrap printer or photocopier paper can be ironed on to fabric. This is useful for fabric painting and appliqué. You can also buy this paper, called **freezer paper**, from quilting suppliers.
◆ Cut out your printed motif and use.

Print on transfer paper.

◆ Design using a paint or draw program.
◆ You may need to adjust the ink intensity within the program. Look at the options in the PRINT menu.
◆ If possible, do a test piece. Sometimes the colours change drastically, and you may need to adjust for this factor.
◆ Iron your printout on to fabric, following the manufacturer's instructions very carefully. Care taken at this stage is the key to success.

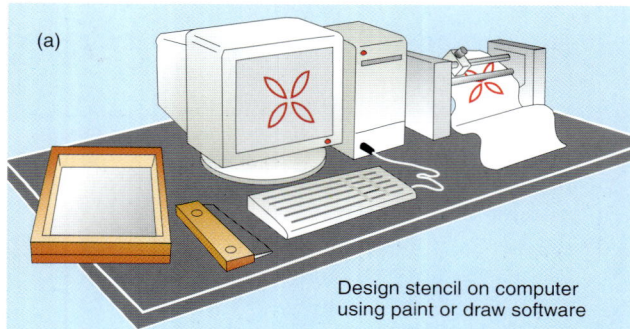

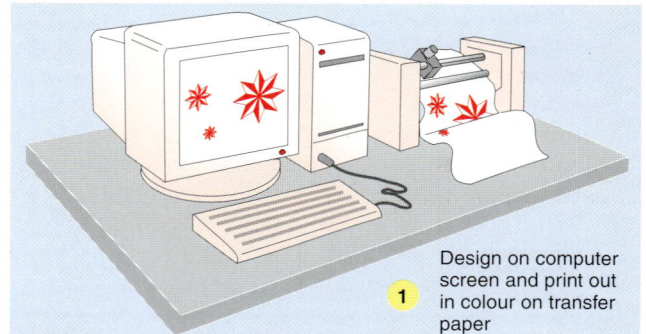

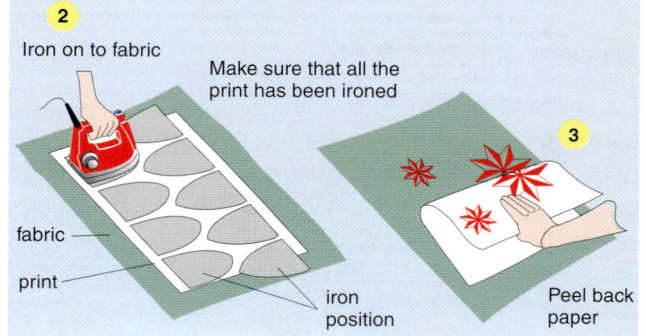

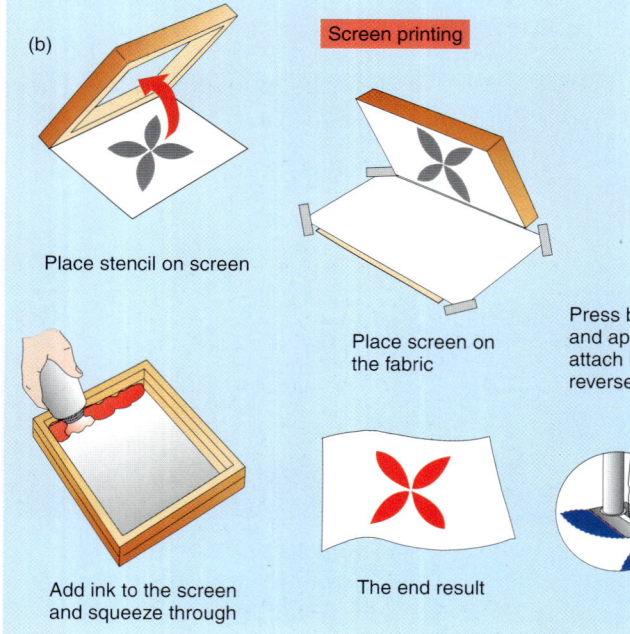

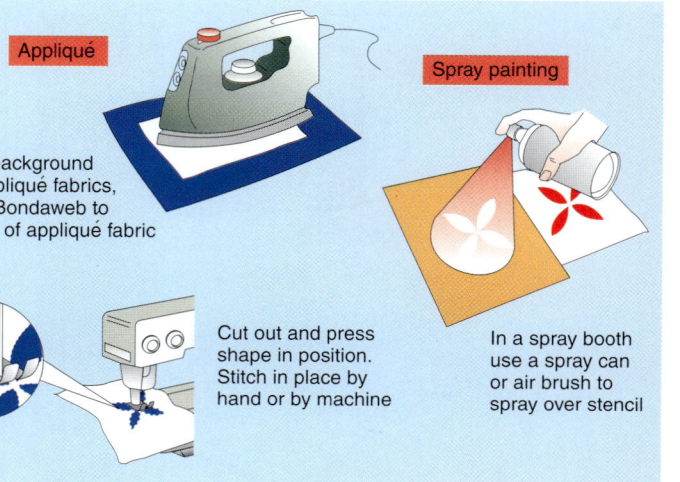

1 Design on computer screen and print out in colour on transfer paper

2 Iron on to fabric
Make sure that all the print has been ironed
fabric
print
iron position

3 Peel back paper

(a) Design stencil on computer using paint or draw software

(b) **Screen printing**
Place stencil on screen
Place screen on the fabric
Add ink to the screen and squeeze through
The end result

Appliqué
Press background and appliqué fabrics, attach Bondaweb to reverse of appliqué fabric
Cut out and press shape in position. Stitch in place by hand or by machine

Spray painting
In a spray booth use a spray can or air brush to spray over stencil

Manufacturing

74

Export to embroidery software.

◆ Save the design as a file in the format suitable for reading by the embroidery software. Size may also be critical – check the requirements of the embroidery software.

◆ Call up the file to the embroidery software.

◆ Using the design as a template, specify the stitches required to make up the stitched design. Depending on the software, this may require the stitches for each area of the design to be chosen specifically, or the software may itself make a 'best guess' at the final result.

◆ Save the file in the format required for stitching. Check the requirements of the embroidery software. This may be on computer disk or on a transferable electronic card.

◆ Connect the embroidery machine or load the card. Stitch out the design.

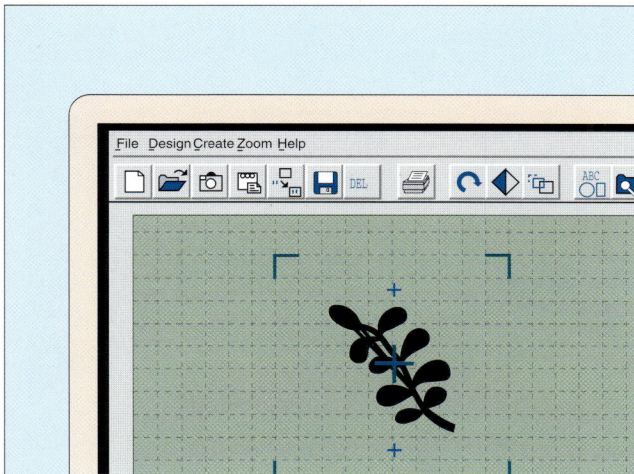

The pattern is designed using computer software. It is digitised so that the sewing machine will output the design in stitches.

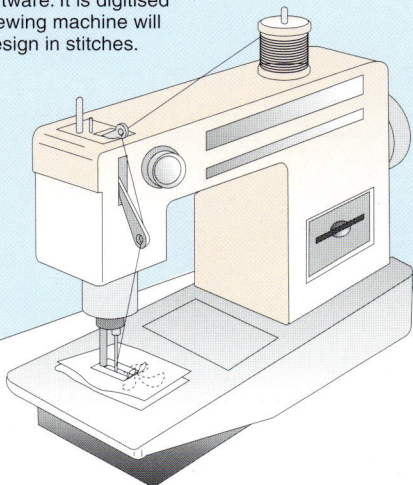

Making a block for printing

◆ Design your block on the computer following the software instructions.

◆ Use a vertical CNC Mill or engraving machine to prepare the block.

◆ Ink the block and prepare to print.

Using software to design woven fabrics

◆ Design your fabric using the software.

◆ Choose the number of yarn colours in the warp and weft to produce a fabric colourway.

◆ Edit the scale of the cloth to suit the textiles end product.

◆ Save the design and use it to develop other fabric ideas or print it out for use on a design sheet or moodboard.

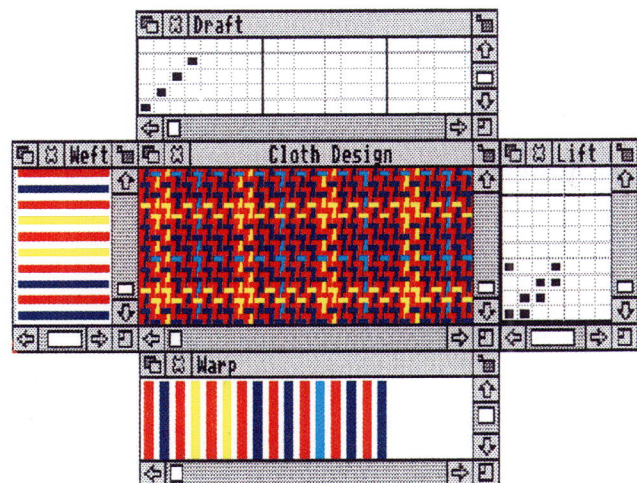

Different methods of production

Lay planning and cutting

A lay plan is where the pattern pieces or templates of all the individual components of a product are laid together in such a way that they fit on the material closely and efficiently to minimise waste. A lot of money can be saved by the efficiency of the lay plan and it is therefore an important part of the manufacturing process, especially when cutting for mass production. To save two or three per cent on a lay may not sound very much until you realise how much fabric that involves.

Fabrics which have to be cut in one direction, such as a pile fabric (like velvet) or a one-way print, are usually very uneconomical. Fabrics which allow the pieces to be laid in both directions will therefore reduce the fabric costs. If the material is knitted or woven, and for leather, plastic or rubber, consideration must be taken as to the grain.

Case study: Speedo

The swimwear manufacturer Speedo uses a CAD system which includes cost-efficient lay plans and markers that are laid out on to 60 layers of fabric in the cutting room. The fabric is then cut automatically by a knife following horizontal and vertical co-ordinates. The system has improved accuracy and efficiency, and cut down on waste fabric.

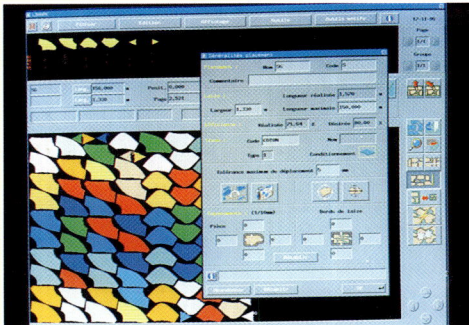

Focused task: Lay plans

Produce a lay plan for your product which shows maximum usage of your material. Measure the width of the material before you start, and draw out the position of the pattern pieces. It may be necessary to lay two or more of the complete product to show full use of the material. This can be done on a computer.

You can quickly estimate how much fabric you need by laying out your pattern pieces on the corner of a large table.

Standard width fabrics (90cm/115cm) are often folded lengthways to make it quicker to cut out two of the same pattern piece.

Try working out the pattern lay for 90cm then see if it is more economical to use 115cm.

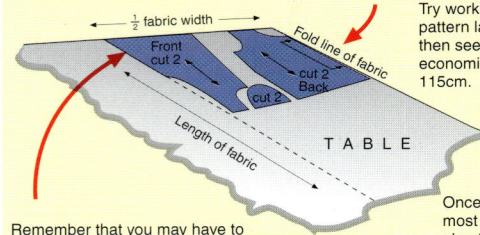

Remember that you may have to place the pattern pieces to follow the grain of the fabric, or match stripes or checks.
· For non-woven fabric lay the pattern in any direction.
· For plain fabric or linings lay the pattern in either direction.
· For fabrics with a directional pattern or pile, or knitted fabrics, lay the pattern in one direction.

Once you have the most economical lay plan transfer your pattern lay to fabric and cut it out.

Case study: D&E Textiles

D&E Textiles provides a specialist cutting service to a wide variety of garment manufacturers, including sportswear companies such as Umbro, Adidas and Reebok. The cutting company has won much acclaim from the industry, including two awards for innovation, marketing and competitiveness.

The quality of a product can be significantly affected by the accuracy of pattern matching. This is a difficult and time-consuming task which can only be executed properly if done manually. Each ply (layer) is spread, matching the pattern exactly at the sides and each end of the lay.

Spreading fabric.

The lay is cut either with a straight knife or using the CAM automatic cutter. Computer-generated 'cut' data can be sent by the customer on disk or using a modem. Companies working JIT systems can save a huge amount of time. A lay that takes 90 minutes to cut with a straight knife will take only ten minutes using the CAM machine.

Matching stripes.

The fabric arrives in batches from the manufacturer, and is then prepared and stacked at the back of the automatic cutters ready for spreading. The operatives spread the fabric automatically, following the instructions on the cutting docket. This will state the depth of the ply (how many layers) and length of the lay. The lay is then 'air flowed' (air is blown under the lay) into position down the cutting table.

After the fabric has been cut it is sorted into bundles and dispatched to the customer.

Different methods of production

Joining techniques

There are different ways of joining fabrics together depending upon the type of materials used, the processes available and the end use of the item. Bonding, stitching, gluing and heat-sealing are the main joining techniques used, with stitching being the most common. When planning the manufacturing process the type of seam finishes required will be given in the work order.

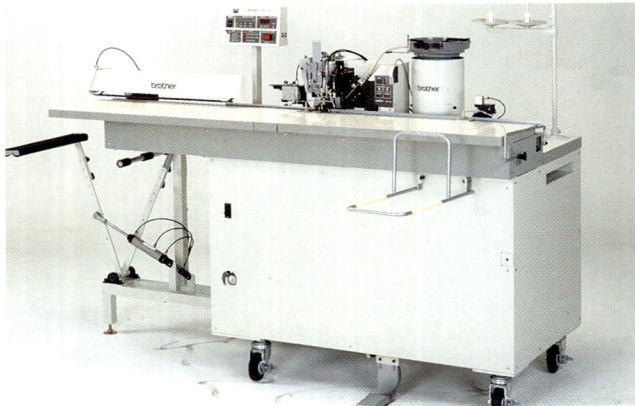

One type of sewing machine used to produce the seams on a denim jacket.

There are many different types of stitching – the British Standard (BS 3870 Part One: 1982) gives 98 standard forms, including lockstitch, overlock, flat-lock, buttonhole and seamcover, and there are many different types of sewing machine. Common seams you will find on textile products are lockstitch, overlock and seamcover.

Lockstitch

Originally hand-sewn, the straight running stitch method of joining fabric is now known as and performed by a 'lockstitch' machine. This is the most common type of joining stitch, with the right side of the fabrics sewn together producing an unfinished seam. The raw edges of the seam can be finished after or during the joining process to prevent fraying and produce a harder wearing, neater and more professional finish, using either a zigzag or overlocker stitch which binds the fabric threads together.

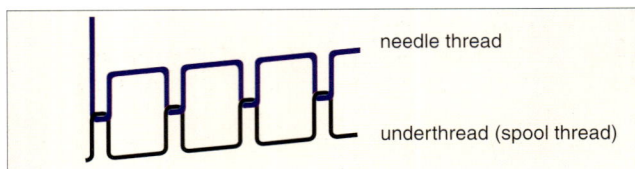

needle thread

underthread (spool thread)

Overlock stitch

Overlocking is a cost-effective method of finishing seams on fabrics that tend to fray. It may be used in conjunction with a lockstitch seam to finish the edges, or it may be used to join two fabrics in one operation. The stitch itself uses either two, three, four or five individual threads in a combination of zigzags and loops.

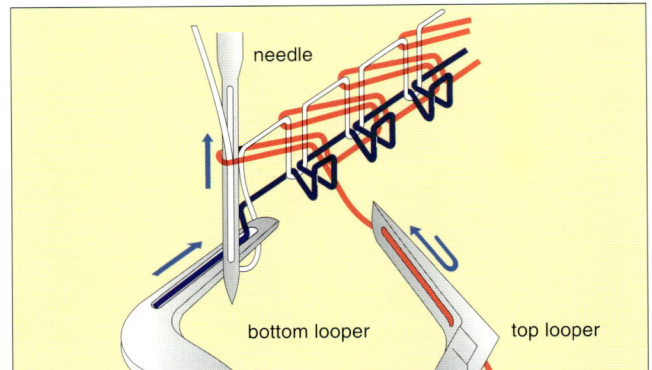

needle

bottom looper   top looper

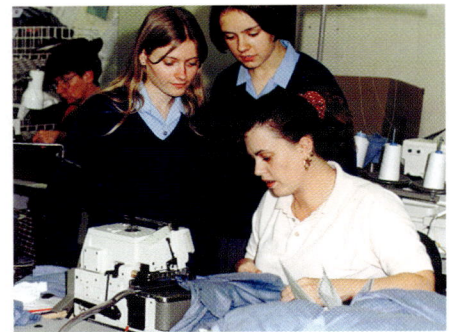

A skilled machinist at Martin Emprex International demonstrates overlocking to Meden School students.

Seamcover stitch

Seamcovering is a versatile stitch using twin needles to create the top stitch and an overlock stitch underneath. It is mostly used to hem garments, especially fabrics which might fray – T-shirts, for example. It can be used with elastic in swimwear.

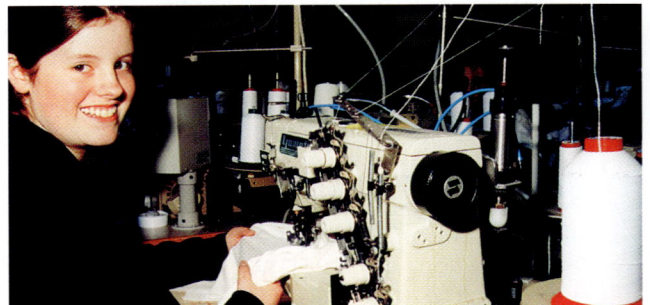

A student from Holgate School is seen using a coverseam machine at Counterpart Clothing to hem her outfit.

Manufacturing

Linking

When joining knitwear together, a linking machine is used to achieve a flat seam. This is a complex process using special machinery which virtually knits the garment pieces together. A very high degree of skill is required to link together the fabric stitch by stitch.

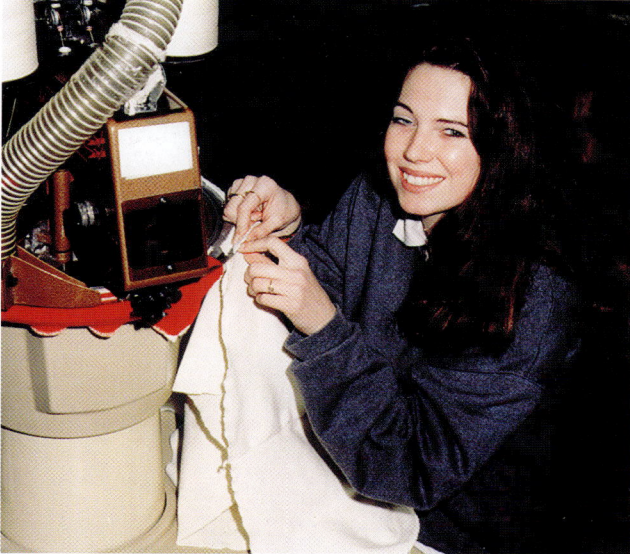

Louise Heaver from Portland School is shown here learning how to link her knitted garment together at Coats Viyella Knitwear.

Finishing

Once the pattern pieces have been joined together, the product needs to be **finished off**, ready for delivery to the customer. This will include making sure there are no loose threads, tying in yarn ends on knitwear, and a thorough final inspection to check for faults or defects. After this inspection the product is pressed, labelled and packaged ready for delivery.

Pressing

This process uses dry heat or steam to press the product into shape, and can be achieved by a combination of the following methods.

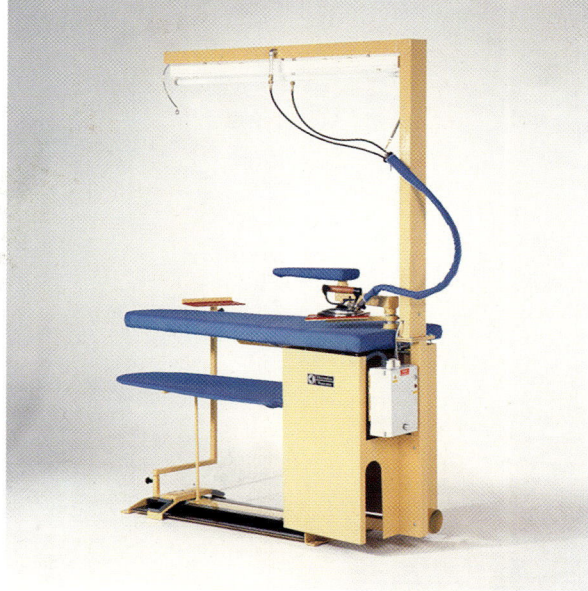

A pressing unit for ironing with a high-pressure steam iron.

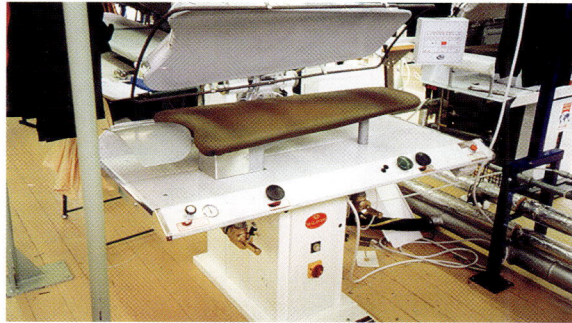

This flat-bed press is a specialised pressing unit in which trousers are pressed flat

---

Focused task: Choosing joining techniques

- Collect together a number of textile products, such as bags, garments and accessories. Examine them closely and identify what joining methods have been used on these products and why. Present your findings as a chart.
- Find examples of textile products that use joining methods other than stitching, such as bonding, gluing and heat-sealing.

What joining techniques would you use for the following textile products?

- To attach a rucksack strap to a the main body.
- To join the side seams of a T-shirt.
- To join the seams of a knitted jumper.
- To join the seams of a knitted car seat cover.
- To join piping or trim to an upholstered settee cover.
- To attach curtain tape to the top of curtains.

Pressing (continued)

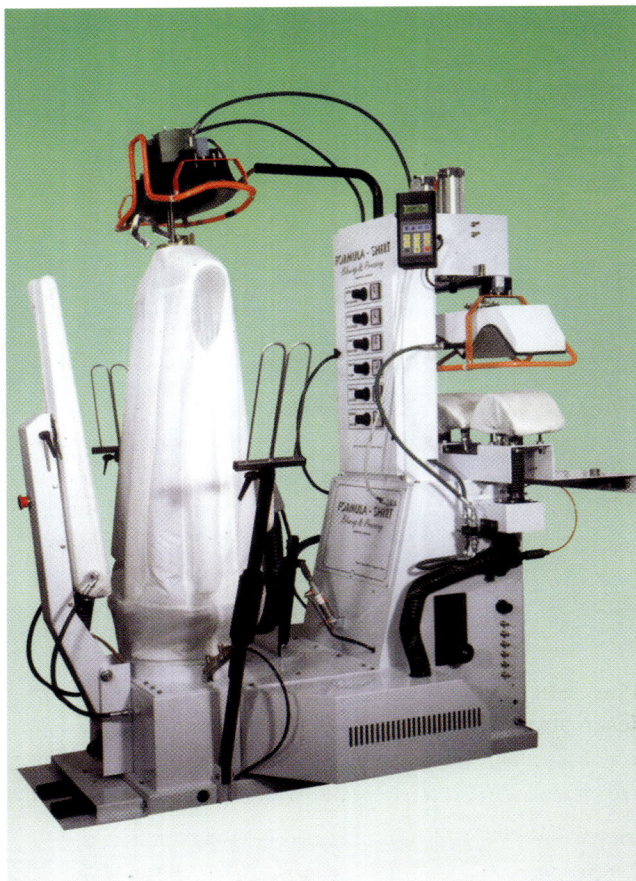

Using a steam dolly, the garment is placed upon a form which is then inflated by blowing with steam and air for several minutes.

Labelling

It is important for every product, once manufactured, to be correctly labelled with the following information.

◆ Sewn-in labelling – a label in the back of the neck of a garment, or fitted into a side seam with information relating to the product size, name of the label or brand, country of origin and fibre composition. It is a legal requirement for all textile products sold within the UK to have the accurate fibre composition marked.
◆ Care instructions – these may appear as part of the label or separately, and provide the consumer with washing and garment aftercare instructions.
◆ Bar code – as each product is completed a bar code will be attached to indicate the product type, size, order number, customer, and manufacturing batch.

Packaging

Once the product has been labelled and pressed it is packaged, ready either to go into stock or for despatch to the customer. Depending upon the nature of the product it may be boxed, wrapped in polythene, put on to hangers, or folded. The aim of the packaging is to protect the product from damage until it reaches the consumer.

Possible problems occur when there is a needle breakage on a machine during the sewing process, as the broken metal may become embedded within the garment. In the case of children's clothing, stringent regulations are placed upon the manufacturer to check that as the garments leave the factory there is no metal present within them. To ensure this does not happen the garments, once packaged, pass through a metal-detecting machine.

This needle detector ensures garments are safe.

Focused task: Labelling

■ Collect labels from garments and list the items which are included on them. Which labels do you find easiest to use and why?
■ Design a label with care instructions for a textile product you have made. Include product size, care instructions, name of brand, country of origin, and accurate fibre composition.

Quality assurance and quality control

To sell goods that don't come back to customers who do.
Littlewoods Home Shopping
Quality Initiative team

Quality is all about meeting a consistent standard for every product manufactured, resulting in identical goods even if they are produced by different people or different factories. The aim of the quality system is to manufacture goods that are all the same with a zero fault rate. However, this is easier said than done, particularly if the company is manufacturing thousands of items of the same product, or even if they are manufacturing a small batch.

Once the product standard has been agreed by the customer, its materials and processes are documented to ensure that each item manufactured conforms to the specification and is identical to the original sample. In other words, it is manufactured right, first time, every time.

Quality control is built into each process, with everybody checking it against the standards as the product is produced. In this way quality becomes everybody's responsibility. At the end of the manufacturing process a thorough inspection is carried out as a final check, and if there is a fault it is spotted and rectified before the product is delivered to the customer.

Quality systems

A quality system is implemented through the writing of a detailed **specification**, the standardisation of procedures, the testing of raw materials, and the regular inspection of the product. Every quality system is concerned with documenting every single material and process that goes to make the product, and a number of critical checks are made at varying stages of manufacture :

Raw materials – such as fabric, threads, and all components – must be checked on arrival, batch by batch, to ensure they are the same as the sample. Remember that in a real factory the designer will not be available to approve the delivery, therefore colour, weight, width, handle and performance must be checked against the specification and original fabric cuttings.

The design specification must provide a clear description of the design of the product, with instructions about technical details such as seam finishes, hem allowances, and tolerances on finished width and length.

Production processes must also be detailed. The cutter must have a set of instructions and the lay plan to ensure the correct fabric is cut the right way around. After cutting each component must be labelled with information, including pattern piece, size, colour, order number and batch number. This may be in the form of a bar code. During making-up, a systematic order of work must be followed using defined sewing techniques, with each joining process being identified in addition to seam allowances and tolerances.

In final inspection the size, fit and overall look of the finished product will be matched against the standard. In the case of a garment this might be a sealed sample in a bag.

Focused task: Quality standards

lifetime guarantee
oversize storm flaps keep rain out
padded back for comfort
all stay-fast lock stitching
thread that matches
completely waterproof fabric
genuine leather reinforced bottom

no guarantee
undersize storm flaps let in rain
chain-stitching
thread that doesn't match
fabric water-resistant only
imitation leather bottom sewed to fabric

These two bags have been manufactured using different sets of quality criteria. Despite having a similar look, the bag on the left has been designed with additional features, and manufactured using superior materials and techniques. How would the quality systems differ between the two bags?

▶ Testing, page 66

Quality assurance and quality control

Standards

Certain types of products must conform to British or European Standards legislation. For instance, children's nightwear must have rigorous procedures for checking flammability, and these are set by external organisations.

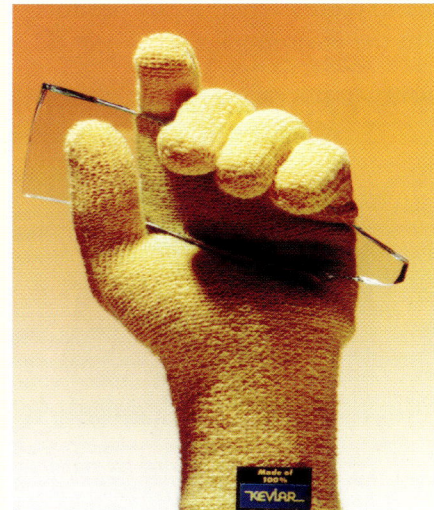

Teamworking in industry

Volume manufacturing of a product usually requires more than one person performing the several stages in its production, so the success of a product relies not just on good design and materials but also on the efficiency of its manufacture. This can only be achieved through **teamworking**. The more efficient the team in meeting quality standards and deadlines, the less waste in time and materials and the higher the profit.

In the textiles industry teamworking can take different forms:

◆ production line arrangements
◆ cellular manufacture.

Cellular manufacture involves between three and six machinists producing complete garments. The whole team is responsible for the quality of each finished garment.

Case study: *Ordsall Hall School working with Coats Viyella Clothing, Retford.*

These students were asked by a local manufacturer to design a range of garments for the teenage market for spring/summer 1997. They formed their own design label, 'Civilisation', and designed a range of garments from which they manufactured one item.

The students are seen here marking the pattern pieces on to the fabric prior to cutting and making-up. In industry this task would normally be performed by one member of the production team, the cutter, who lays out and cuts the fabric. To mass produce the garment the cutter would lay many lengths of the fabric on top of each other and cut in one go.

▶ **Lay planning and cutting page 76**

MANUFACTURING

83

Teamworking in industry

Focused task: Teamworking

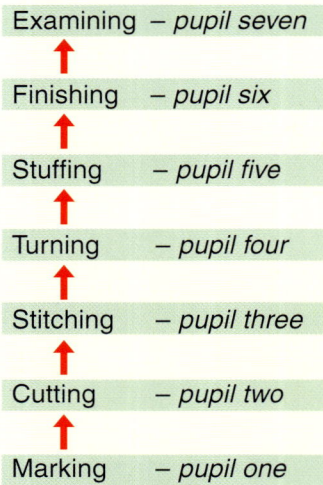

Examining – *pupil seven*

↑

Finishing – *pupil six*

↑

Stuffing – *pupil five*

↑

Turning – *pupil four*

↑

Stitching – *pupil three*

↑

Cutting – *pupil two*

↑

Marking – *pupil one*

Line Production
one operation per team member

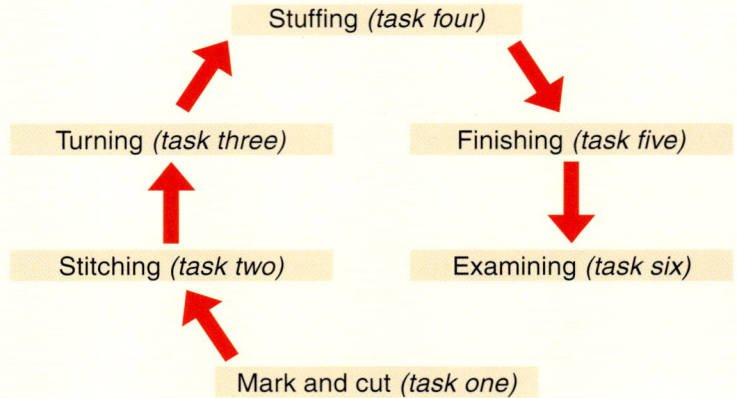

Stuffing *(task four)*

Turning *(task three)* → Finishing *(task five)*

Stitching *(task two)* → Examining *(task six)*

Mark and cut *(task one)*

Cell Production
multi-skilled operatives

This activity will give an understanding of working in teams and the difference between a production line and cellular manufacture.

In groups of no more than six or seven you are asked to mass produce a juggling ball or similar simple product. Before you start you will need to do the following:

■ produce a template from which the product will be cut
■ work out the different processes in the manufacture of the product and produce a work order (production plan)
■ produce a manufacturing specification to check against as you work
■ decide on a time limit in which to produce one or more of the product.

First, simulate a production line. Allocate one or more of the production processes to each team member, and produce as many products as you can in the time allowed.

Second, simulate a cell. The fabric pieces are pre-cut, and each team member produces one complete product in the time allowed.

Thirdly, do a final check of each product against the manufacturing specifications for quality standards. Those not meeting the required standards are rejected. Evaluate the different methods of working to produce the same quantity of one product to the same standards.

Do the right thing!

• Plan the processes well to save time.
• For the production line, decide who would be best for each task.
• Plan the time allowed for each process.
• Organise the equipment to save time and ensure ease of use and safety.
• Work to meet agreed quality standards.
• Use continuous inspection to control quality.

Systems and control in the textiles industry

Volume knitting production

Knitted textiles are formed from a continuous length of yarn which has been made into loops, or stitches, connected to one another. Many thousands of loops knitted together may be needed to produce a finished garment.

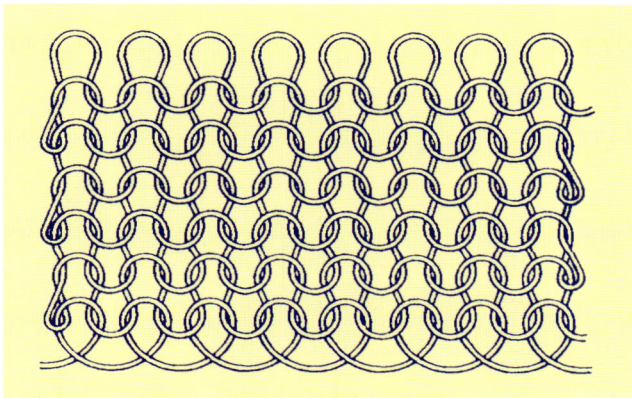

This diagram shows a series of uniform stitches all going in the same direction

Hand knitting is very time-consuming, or **labour-intensive**, so we usually use machines. Since the first knitting machine, a stocking frame invented by William Lee in 1589, there have been many improvements to knitting machines.

There are three methods of producing knitted products in high volume.

1   Cut-and-sew blanket knitting – rolls of knitted fabric are produced, and then cut to shape and sewn to make the product.

Shape knitting is being used here to manufacture the individual parts of these garments prior to assembly.

2   Shape knitting – the individual components of products are knitted to shape, so avoiding waste.
3   3D knitting – whole products are created in one piece, with no sewing or linking.

This sweater is a seamless knitted structure and has been developed as a result of the latest WholeGarment technology.

Focused task: Development of knitting

- Why has knitting developed in this way?
- What advantages might be gained from seamless knitting?
- Can you think of new products, other than garments, that could be made in this way?

Focused task: *Properties of knitted structures*

Many different kinds of products, besides garments, can be knitted. Designers and manufacturers are developing new kinds of knitted products.

- Compare knitted textiles with other kinds of materials.
- What are the special properties that knitted structures provide?
- Make a chart to explain your findings.

Each of these products benefits from the special properties that knitted structures provide.

The industrial knitting machine

Modern industrial knitting machines can be fully automated and will knit complex products in minutes, direct from the designer's concept drawing. They can also repeat each process accurately for volume production of the same item.

> ▶ **D&T Routes Core Book,**
> **Volumes of production**
> **page 120**

Computer-controlled knitting machines use CAD/CAM to control stitch pattern, colours, shape and design of the final product very precisely. Using powerful computerised design systems, the designer can also model the knit in virtual reality before manufacturing starts. The sweater on the previous page is a virtual reality (VR) image.

Systems and control in knitting

For the knitting machine to manufacture a seamless product successfully, many possible variables have to be controlled. For example, a digital stitch control system (DSCS) regulates every loop in the knitted structure. Digital checking of each one makes sure it is the same when connected to its neighbour.

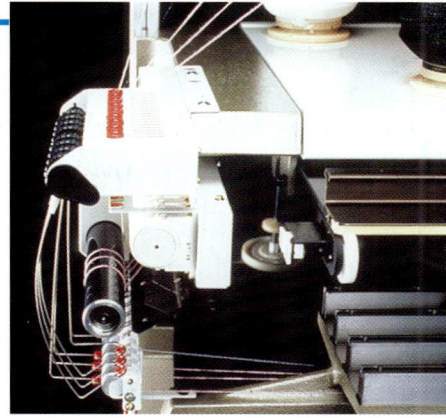

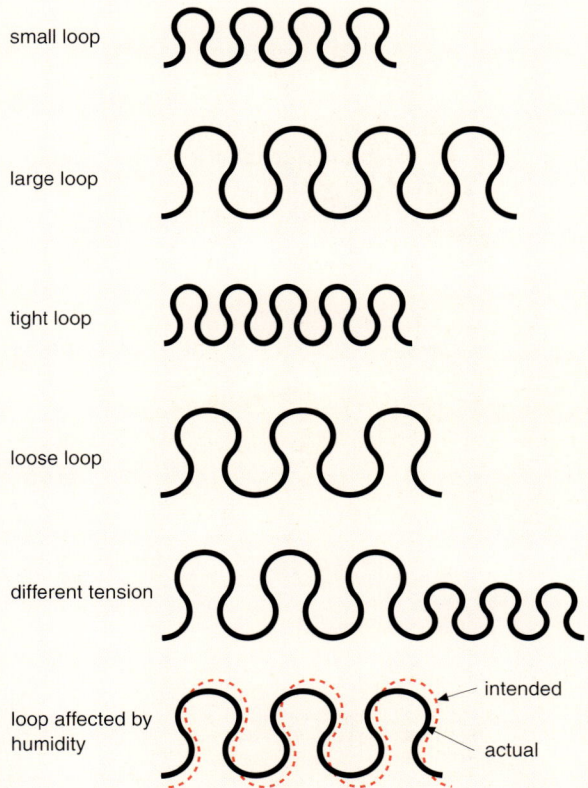

small loop

large loop

tight loop

loose loop

different tension

loop affected by humidity → intended → actual

Each of these loops is different. In a perfect knitted structure their differences must be eliminated.

DSCS is a good example of a **feedback** or **closed-loop control system**. This can be represented using a systems diagram showing the input, processing and output stages.

In DSCS the yarn feed and tension is automatically adjusted, allowing knitting with continuously stable loop length. The DSCS monitors any changes in temperature, humidity, dyeing and tension strength, and makes adjustments automatically. Every garment produced will conform to the specification, with a tolerance of within plus-or-minus one per cent.

a) In a system a process produces the required outputs in response to the inputs it receives. This system has no feedback – once it has been started it will continue without taking any account of what is actually happening to the output. This type of system is known as an **open-loop control system**.

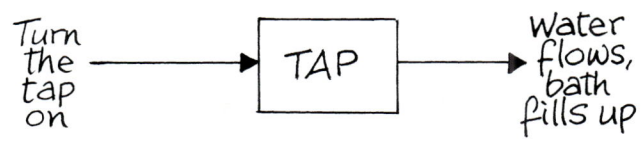

Turn the tap on → TAP → Water flows, bath fills up

b) In this **closed-loop** system, information is fed back from the output. This information is used to monitor or control the system, to keep the output at the required level or make sure it is doing what was intended.

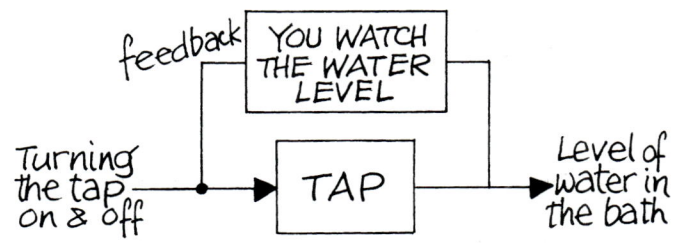

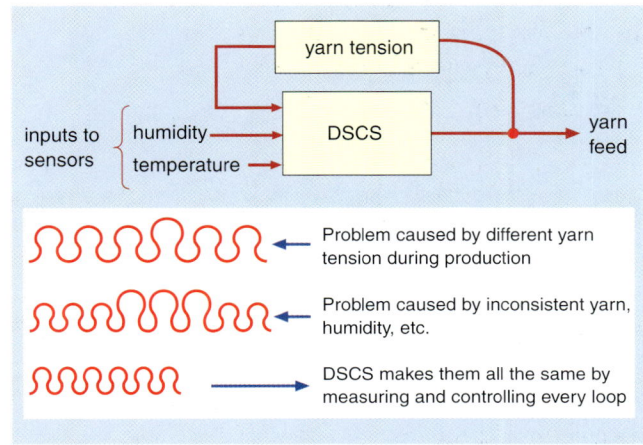

feedback | YOU WATCH THE WATER LEVEL

Turning the tap on & off → TAP → Level of water in the bath

yarn tension

inputs to sensors { humidity, temperature } → DSCS → yarn feed

Problem caused by different yarn tension during production

Problem caused by inconsistent yarn, humidity, etc.

DSCS makes them all the same by measuring and controlling every loop

The key features of the DSCS control system. This also shows how electronics or microprocessors are used to control other types of system, such as mechanical systems.

Focused task: Investigating control systems

You can use kits to set up and investigate control systems quickly and easily. In this task you will use an electronics kit or a microprocessor (this could be a computer) to model part of the DSCS system described on page 87. You will find out how a sensor can be used to monitor changes in temperature, and how this information can be processed to control a mechanical system.

You will need an electronics systems kit or a microprocessor – your teacher may need to give you some lessons in how to use these, or you may have learned in your KS3 course. The parts of the kit you will need are:

- ■ a temperature sensor – this is the **input** sensor, and will provide information for the process unit
- ■ an input voltage unit – this will be used to **programme** the system or set the level you want for the system
- ■ an electric motor to act as a mechanical **output** – this could be used with either yarn feed or tension control when attached to other mechanical systems

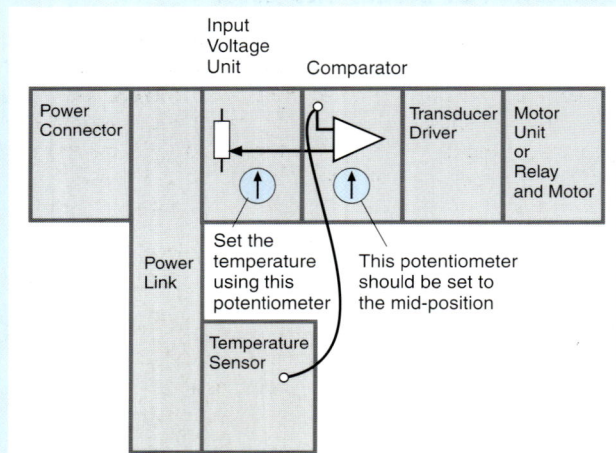

- ■ a transducer driver – this enables the motor to be driven from the process unit
- ■ a comparator – this will be the process unit for your system
- ■ a power supply for the system.

Investigate what happens when the temperature changes; you can do this by warming the temperature sensor with your fingers. Explain how the system works, using the expressions:

- • input
- • output
- • process
- • sensor.

Explain how this system would could be used to take account of temperature changes using the DSCS system. How could you add feedback to this system to produce a closed-loop control system? Try using different sensors and output devices to model other parts of the DSCS system.

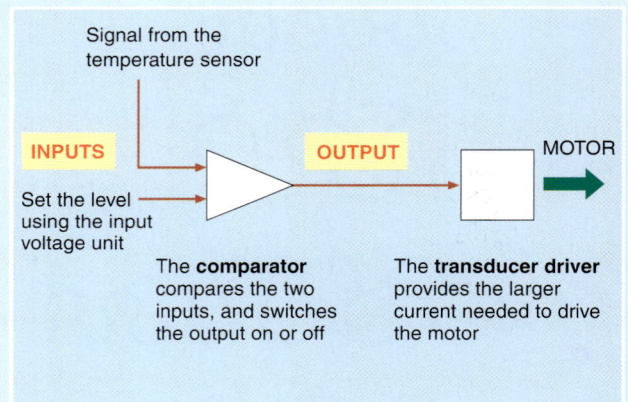

This shows how the system should be assembled.

This shows how the system works.

▶ **D&T Routes Control Products** Control systems, page 36

Focused task: Controlling knitted products

Systems and control, through DSCS, has helped improve machine-knitted products. DSCS has also allowed manufacturers to predict more accurately:

- ■ the quantity of yarn needed for the number of products to be manufactured
- ■ the weight of yarn needed for a particular design
- ■ the accuracy of knitted shapes.

Being able to control knitted structures as they are formed, through systems, has improved quality of the product, reduced the number of stages needed for manufacture and increased the reliability of the manufacturing processes.

- ■ What are the benefits of this to customers?
- ■ What are the benefits of this to manufacturers?

Answer these two questions, in the form of a short study, for homework.

The use of new technologies

Scope – Lycra suit

Scope is a charity working with people who have cerebral palsy, a physical condition which leaves muscles hard to control. This makes it difficult to communicate or get around. New trials using Lycra garments to support muscles have been successful, and led to a larger study on children with cerebral palsy. The result is a new type of Lycra suit which provides support and comfort for muscles while allowing easy movement – the suit is said to be "dynamic". The photograph shows Pasha Thompson wearing her Lycra suit, which has improved her muscle control and given her a new independence.

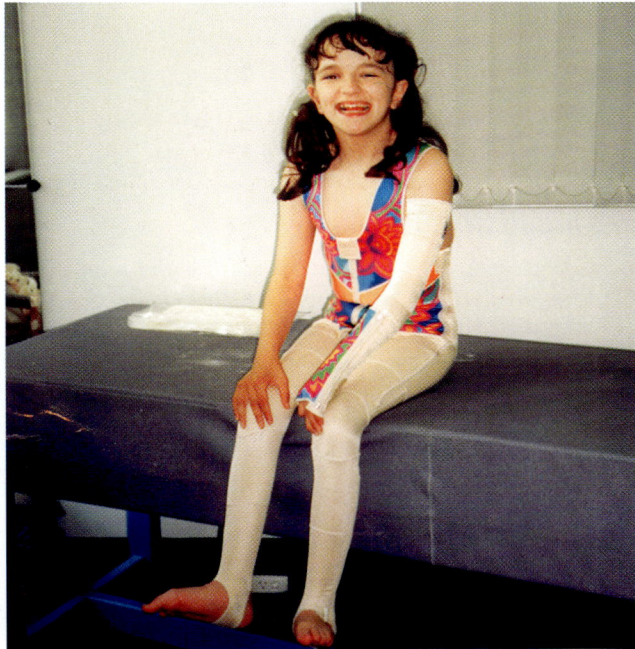

Sun-protective clothing

Each year over 1000 Australians die from skin cancer, and over two-thirds of all Australians will have some form of skin cancer during their lives. Textile products do not offer 100 per cent protection against the harmful ultraviolet rays from the sun, but could if modified. Researchers in Australia are developing new fibres and technologies to do just this. Once developed, the researchers are hoping to establish a standard that informs the consumer as to the sun protection factor of the particular garment.

Virtual reality catwalk

Researchers at leading universities are currently developing CAD systems that will not only allow the designer the opportunity to produce virtual garments, but also the opportunity of staging a virtual fashion show. In this show computer-animated graphics simulate three-dimensionally the model walking down the catwalk wearing the new garment ideas. It also has applications within home textiles, with designers being able to co-ordinate whole room interiors without making one sample product.

New fibre developments

With about one-third of its European fibre sales going into technical applications, DuPont has one of the widest product ranges of any fibre producer. The company produces a wide variety of textile fibres, from Lycra through to Kevlar. DuPont's Kevlar is being used in cables in a new civil engineering technique called **modular compression engineering**. The cables maintain permanent compression of horizontal or inclined planar structures, such as bridges and roofs.

Recycling PET bottles into fleece

Think twice before throwing away plastic bottles! Companies are now recycling them and making them into a range of products, such as fibre-fill for duvets and anoraks, strapping for packaging, and fleece fabric for jackets, sweaters and so on. It takes about 25 plastic bottles to make one sweater.

Austen Constable designed this jacket having seen a display about recycling plastic bottles.

The use of new technologies

3D textiles

Developments in the way fabrics are constructed has led to a breakthrough in producing 3D textiles that are knitted, woven or braided to form structures without any type of joining being required. This has led to the discovery of a whole new area for textile products. Some of the most exciting recent developments have included:

- parts for a Rolls Royce jet engine which are 100 per cent knitted in silicon carbon
- contoured seat covers from Teknit
- the pre-form for a rocket motor exit cone, made entirely out of braided fibres.

A rocket motor exit cone (shown left) is being braided by this machine.

The fabrics of tomorrow

Research into materials for the year 2000 reveals some unusual products.

- A blouse which smells of roses – the manufacturing process locks fragrant microcapsules into the fabric which gradually release their scent.
- A green jacket which turns blue according to the weather – liquid crystals in coated fabrics or thermochromic dyes allow colours of fabrics to change according to the temperature.
- Clothes in pineapple leaf fibres.

Aseptic fibre: RHOVYL® – the end of smelly socks!

By introducing an antibacterial substance in the production process, RHOVYL has developed an aseptic fibre. It forms a natural barrier against bacteria growing and is unchanging throughout the life of the product, despite successive washings. This fibre is good for underwear, sportswear, socks and so on. It can also be used in places requiring strict hygiene, such as hospitals, hotels, public transport, and food processing plants.

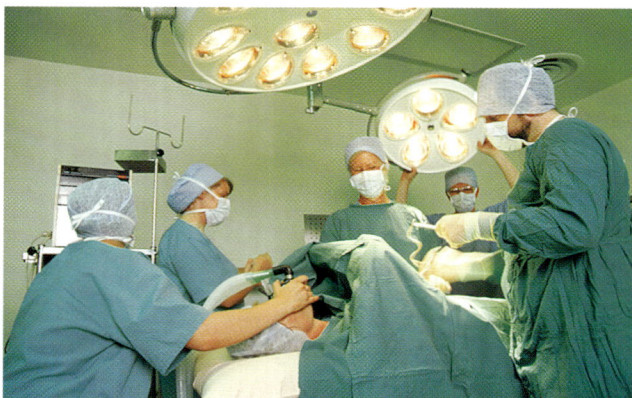

The impact of biotechnology

Biotechnology can be used to produce new or modified fibres, as well as improving the production yields of existing ones. Here are some examples:

- Cotton plants can be made less vulnerable to insects.
- Growing coloured cottons could one day replace the need for bleaches and dyes.
- Sheep have been bred to shed their wool in one piece instead of needing shearing!
- The US Army is trying to develop spider silk as a high-performance fibre for use in bulletproof vests.
- The use of microbial enzymes has begun to expand, replacing existing chemical or mechanical processes like bleaching and scouring.

Waste treatment is probably the biggest industrial application of biotechnology. It can be used in new production processes that are less polluting than traditional ones, such as colour removal from dye-house effluent.

Made to measure – Levi's Personal Pair™

Computer technology and quick-response manufacturing will make it possible for you to have your clothes designed and made to your personal preference but without costing the earth. Levi's can combine computer programming and a consumer's body specifications to develop a customised pair of jeans for a customer. Three weeks later they are delivered. Additional orders are available through an individualised bar code sewn in the label.

MANUFACTURING

There is more to a company than a product and a production line. Somebody has to organise the company, employ and train staff, pay wages, process orders, find buyers, arrange deliveries and so on. It is not enough for a company to manufacture a good product. Managing the different parts of a business properly means getting the **right quantity** of the **right product** to the **right place** at the **right time** to sell at the right price.

Who are the manufacturers?

Different kinds of manufacturing are located in every region of the United Kingdom.

Sectors of manufacturing that use textiles and clothing make up 5.7% of the whole. The case study that follows is to help you understand the variety of work that takes place within a manufacturing company. You might compare it with case studies from other sectors of manufacturing contained in the other *D&T Routes* Focus Area books to develop a broader picture.

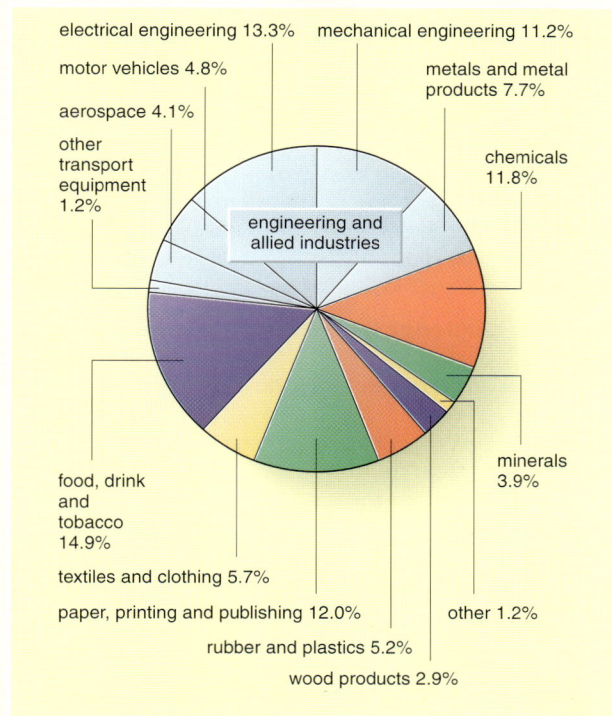

electrical engineering 13.3%   mechanical engineering 11.2%
motor vehicles 4.8%   metals and metal products 7.7%
aerospace 4.1%   chemicals 11.8%
other transport equipment 1.2%
engineering and allied industries
minerals 3.9%
food, drink and tobacco 14.9%
textiles and clothing 5.7%
paper, printing and publishing 12.0%   other 1.2%
rubber and plastics 5.2%
wood products 2.9%

This chart shows the relative size of different sectors manufacturing different types of products.

Case study: Welbeck UK

Welbeck UK produces fashion and technical textiles for specialised areas of the textile market. Its customers include leading UK and international companies. It has four divisions:

- **Welbeck Fabrics** makes high-quality knitted fabrics for use in lingerie and activewear
- **Welbeck Technical** produces highly-specialised technical fabrics, including geotextiles
- **Welbeck Lace** produces stretch lace, used in lingerie and hosiery for the fashion market, and rigid lace for home furnishings
- **Welbeck Fabric Dyers** dyes and finishes fabrics made by Welbeck and other manufacturers.

Traditional skills and modern technology
The Welbeck plants are located in traditional textile areas. Welbeck Fabrics and Technical are found near Mansfield, which has a long history of knitting, while Welbeck Lace is in Nottingham, an area which has been making lace since the 1700s. In textiles, it is important to have a skilled labour force available.
What is special about Welbeck is that it blends these traditional skills with the latest technological developments to create exciting new fabrics. Sophisticated CAD equipment is used to aid design, and the machines used for manufacturing the textiles are

computer-controlled. The company is at the leading edge of textile manufacture.

Innovation and flexibility
Welbeck uses the latest technologies as part of a process of **continuous improvement**. It is constantly innovating with the latest performance yarns, like **Tactel**, and experimenting with various blends, including metallic yarn, to create exciting fabrics. It uses natural yarns like cotton or manufactured yarns like Lycra to create the feel and the look the customer wants while having the technical characteristics (such as strength and stretchiness) required.

Welbeck uses the most up-to-date computer-controlled machinery (CAM) to produce its fabrics quickly. This gives the management all-important flexibility. They can use a machine for knitting fine fabric for underwear one day and a technical fabric for outdoor wear the next, or even a geotextile. This means they can respond quickly to customers' needs and utilise the machinery efficiently. It is this combination of flexibility and innovation that keeps Welbeck ahead of its competitors and a world leader in textiles.

Meeting challenges – technical textiles

How does Welbeck develop new technical fabrics?

In your D&T work you are given challenges to meet and problems to solve. You have to use your designing and making skills to meet these challenges. Welbeck Technical does much the same in its work. Clothing manufacturers want fabrics which meet the needs of their customers – perhaps for protection in hazardous circumstances or extreme conditions.

Protective 'chaps' made of Kevlar fabric give light-weight, flexible protection for chainsaw users.

To meet these challenges Welbeck uses specialised yarns and its special knitting skills to create fabrics with high specifications. The company's designers work with the designers of the clothing companies to achieve the desired results. For example, fabric for protecting people working with chainsaws has notoriously been heavy and unpleasant to wear. Welbeck's challenge was to produce a lighter-weight fabric which gave increased flexibility without reducing its ability to protect the wearer. Not only did it meet this challenge, but the fabric it developed has set new standards in this field.

Welbeck works with a range of high-specification materials like **Kevlar** and **carbon fibre** to produce fabrics which give strength, heat and chemical resistance. The potential for the use of these is enormous – the textiles industry has an exciting future!

Geotextiles

Some of the most exciting developments in the technical field have taken place in **geotextiles**. These are fabrics which are used in large-scale engineering works to stabilise land: they bond with soil to stop it moving or slipping.

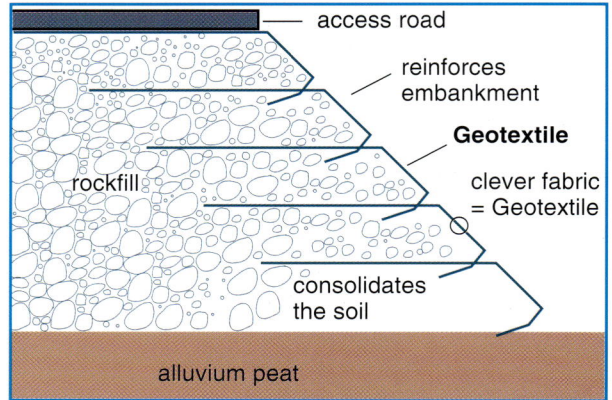

access road

reinforces embankment

Geotextile

clever fabric = Geotextile

rockfill

consolidates the soil

alluvium peat

Geotextiles can be used to strengthen embankments, consolidate land around the bases of bridges, prevent roads cracking or sinking, and reclaim land.

Why geotextiles?

Geotextiles often replace steel and concrete in civil engineering: for example, they could replace a concrete retaining wall to keep soil from slipping on to a motorway. They have many advantages.

- They can be made in different **strengths** – the strongest are stronger than steel. This makes them cost-effective: you manufacture the geotextile to the strength you need for the job, so the costs are lower.
- They can be manufactured in different **ways** to do particular jobs.
- They allow for **filtration** so that water seeps but the soil is not allowed through.
- They are **easier** to lay down than steel and concrete, and can be more **flexible** so they don't crack.

Manufacturing geotextiles

Geotextiles can be manufactured in different ways. They can be knitted, woven or non-woven (bonded by heat or stitch-bonded). Woven and knitted geotextiles are used for soil reinforcement, while non-woven geotextiles are used for filtration and separation of soils. Welbeck uses a special process called **weft insertion knitting** which makes the resultant geotextiles stronger and resistant to tearing. Geotextiles can be combined to give strength and filtration.

The best yarns

The strength and quality of the geotextiles depends on the yarn used and the way they are made. Welbeck uses high-tenacity polyester yarn. The strength can be varied in several ways:

- using thicker yarn (it comes in different counts)
- using more warp ends and setting them closer together
- using more weft picks and setting them closer together.

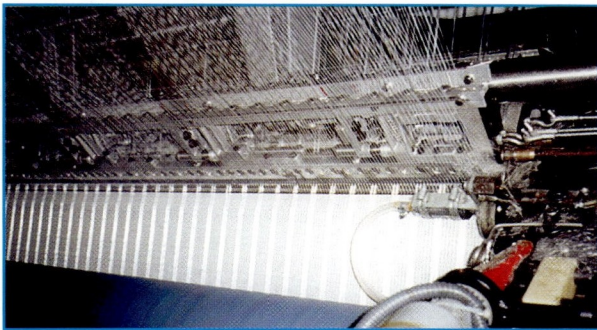

The yarn which forms the warp is fed into the knitting machine from the bobbins on the frame. You can see how many there are. The weft is fed in from the side. It takes a great deal of skill to set up this machine so that the sett is correct and the resulting geotextile is of the desired strength and quality. The machines are computer-controlled. The finished geotextile is collected on the large rolls at the end.

Working with customers to find solutions

Welbeck offers its customers a 'bespoke' service. This means that it works closely with them to ensure that they get the geotextiles that meet their requirements. Welbeck produces geotextiles in certain standard strengths, but these may not be what is exactly needed for a particular job. Using a geotextile that is too strong may waste a lot of money.

Once a project is started, a Welbeck geotextile engineer will go to the work site to examine the soils and the nature of the problem. The engineer works out what sorts of geotextile will be needed and their specifications. For example, the specialist can calculate what strength will be needed to stop an embankment of a particular height from slipping.

How Welbeck works with its customers on projects.

Concept Consider the location of the project and identify problems.
Design Welbeck design service works with client's designers to find solutions.
On site Carry out tests and see if standard Welbeck geotextiles will work or if 'bespoke' textiles are required.
On-site operations Carry out trials with specified geotextiles on the site. Then supervise the laying of the geotextiles to make sure they are not damaged and are laid correctly.
Flexibility Make changes during the installation of the geotextiles if this is required.
Successful completion of project ensuring client satisfaction.

The challenge: To build an embankment on soft soil to reclaim land from the sea for a community park. The embankment would be landscaped with vegetation. The main problems would be making sure the soft soil was stabilised and that the embankment would not slip into the salt-marsh.

The solution: Using Welbeck knitted geotextiles on the bottom to consolidate the soil, to allow filtration but not let the soil through, with a different strength higher up to add extra stability. Then using the right strength geotextiles to reinforce the embankment to stop it moving. Topsoil could be added for landscaping.

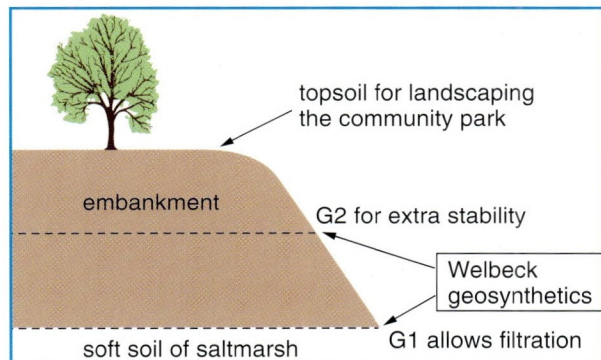

93

Index

2D/3D modelling 59
3D textiles 90

activewear 18
anti-bacterial finish 50
appliqué 26, 56
architectural fabrics 38

bar code labelling 80
belt design 12
biostoning 50
biotechnology 90
breathability 19
business of manufacturing 91

CAD/CAM programs 8, 73
calendering 50
care labelling 47, 80
catwalk, virtual reality 89
characteristics, fabrics 6, 14, 19, 51
chemical properties 50
choice of fabric 13–15, 52
clothing 16, 17, 22, 36, 89
coatings of fabrics 19
colour in design 43
    stability 19
comfort clothes 36
computer design
    equipment 75
    printing 74
    software 8, 75
    spreadsheets 14
computer-generated fabrics 58
consumer demand 36
control systems 87
cost analysis 14, 19, 44, 63
critical path plan 69
cultural influences 5, 30, 37, 40
custom-made product 71
cycle-wear 16–20

data management 69
demand, consumer 36
design 34
    CAD 8, 73
    colour 43
    and culture 30
    evaluation 9
    fabric 6
    fashion 20
    functional 42
    ideas 9
    influences 4, 5, 30, 37, 40
    for manufacture 60
    research 57
    specification 62
    style 43

for testing 68
    themes 6, 38
disassembly 39
distressing fabrics 54
dyeing 55

eco labelling 46
embroidery 55
    software 75
enterprise venture 32
European legislation 82
evaluating fabrics 9, 70
    designs 9

fabric, architectural 38
    choice 13–15, 52
    computer-generated 58
    costings 19
    design 6
    distressing 54
    dyeing 55
    finishes 25, 43, 50, 78
    fire-resistant 50
    flammability 67
    fluorescent 19
    functional 17
    industrial 28
    mood 4
    properties 6, 19, 50, 51
    prototype 4, 9
    reflective 19
    sculpting 55
    special performance 28
    stiffening 51
    survey 6
    technology 3
    testing 51, 66–68
    types 6
fabrics, comfort 36
    situational 37
    smart 28
    technical 28
    with a message 24
fashion design 20
felt 56
fibre content 19
fibres 34, 48, 49, 89, 90
finish, fabric 25, 34, 70, 50
fitness for purpose 47
flammability 67
fluorescent fabrics 19

geotextiles 92

health and safety 45, 47
heat treatment 51

ideas generation 9, 36, 38, 40
image influences 5
industrial fabrics 28

jobbing 71
joining techniques 78

just in time production 70

knitting 85–87

labelling 46, 47, 80
legislation 82
life expectancy 47
lifestyle influences 5
lockstitch 78

made-to-measure products 90
maintenance 47
manufacturing (see production)
market appeal 17
    demand 36
    research 18
materials (see also fabrics)
    manufacturing 63
    raw 48
mercering 50
message in fabrics 24
modelling 14, 59
mola 56
monitoring production 69
mood fabrics 4
moodboards 6, 38

needs assessment 13

packaging 80
performance checklist 18
    testing 66–68
physical properties 50
plan, production 70
pollution control 5
presentation 61
pressing 78
pricing 44
printing by computer 74
processes 63
product life 47
production 62–64
    batch 15, 71
    business 63
    continuous 71
    costs 14, 44, 63
    just in time 70
    mass 71
    materials 63
    methods 71
    monitoring 69
    planning 69, 70
    processes 63
    skills 63
    specification 64
    volume 63, 72
properties, fabrics 6, 19, 50, 51
protective wear 45
prototype fabrics 4, 9

quality 32, 63, 81, 82

raw materials 48
recycling 46, 89
reflective materials 19
regulations 82
research 12, 57
    market 18

safety issues 45, 47
    clothing 16
sculpting 55
simulated testing 68
skills 63
smart fabrics 28
social factors 37
software, computer 8
    embroidery 75
sourcing 62
specification chart 7
    checklist 63
    design 62
    formulation 53
    manufacturing 64
    quality 81
sportswear 18
stability, colour 19
standards 82
stiffening fabrics 51
stitching 78
stonewashing 50
stretch properties 19
style 43
surface finish 25, 50
survey of textiles 6
survival clothing 22
synthetics 48

target group 15
teamwork 83
technical fabrics 28
technology of textiles 3, 89
testing 51, 66, 67
    simulated 68
textile materials (see fabrics)
themes in design 6, 38
traditional dress 31
types of fabric 6

user group 15
    research 18
    needs 13
UV protection 21

virtual reality catwalk 89

water repellency 19
weight of fabrics 19
work orders 70

yarns 49